A Love Story

BETWEEN

2 Worlds

A Love Story
BETWEEN
2 Worlds

Charlie Lord

iUniverse

A LOVE STORY BETWEEN 2 WORLDS

iUniverse books may be ordered through booksellers or by contacting:

iUniverse
1663 Liberty Drive
Bloomington, IN 47403
www.iuniverse.com
844-349-9409

Because of the dynamic nature of the Internet, any web addresses or links contained in this book may have changed since publication and may no longer be valid. The views expressed in this work are solely those of the author and do not necessarily reflect the views of the publisher, and the publisher hereby disclaims any responsibility for them.

Any people depicted in stock imagery provided by Getty Images are models, and such images are being used for illustrative purposes only.
Certain stock imagery © Getty Images.

ISBN: 978-1-6632-5827-4 (sc)
ISBN: 978-1-6632-5826-7 (e)

Library of Congress Control Number: 2023922200

Print information available on the last page.

iUniverse rev. date: 11/17/2023

Contents

Contents

Dedication

I would like to dedicate this book to the memory of Peggy, my wife of many lives;

And to my wife of this life, Danette;

And to my parents, Phil and June Lord, the best parents of any lifetime!

Preface

By Ellen Nikki Wirth

It was a beautiful spring day when my phone rang for the first time to speak with a life-changing force of the fates! I answered the phone to say my little spiel thanking fold for calling me on the psychic line I was on duty for at the time. I was met with a sweet voice of familiar energy that immediately lit up my soul. A lovely lady with brown shoulder-length hair appeared to me in my mediumship abilities from the other side as soon as Charlie began to speak. "Hello! This is Charles Lord out in Topeka, Kansas. Thank you for speaking with me and helping me today." That was what I first remember Charlie ever saying to me. "How can I be of service to you?" I asked Charlie. Peggy began to smile at me in the ethers, she knew that we were about to start an incredible soul journey to remembering our past lives as a twin flame connection turned divine as Peggy had begun to tap Charlie from the other side.

Charlie began to explain to me his profound experience of seeing Peggy as he was hiking on a trail close to his birthday that year. I was there to confirm what Peggy looked like without him telling me. I was there to help him understand the experiences he was having with Peggy. Peggy was his college sweetheart who went in another direction as Charlie did in school. Yet the twin flame connection from several lifetimes was about to be the most divine connection they have known and one of the most divine I have ever encountered in my own work as a psychic medium.

What Peggy and Charlie have taught me is valuable to the collective consciousness. First thing was that all twin flames come into our experiences to clear our karmic debt. They are here for many purposes however the main one is to be of total aid to bring Divinity to our karmic souls.

Charlie and I have talked at least once a week since the very first encounter we had in the spring of 2020. There's been a lot of ground covered in these sessions which we have spent lots of time and effort to gain.

In one of our sessions about a year into this journey I started to see terrible things in my visions. I knew I was a little girl named Olga in an encampment. I knew Peggy was not Peggy in this lifetime but still the same Peggy. I could feel that she was my mother as Olga! This vision didn't stop there. Charlie was my father who I feel was named of Joseph. We were all Jewish in my vision. I was holding on as a young child to Peggy screaming for my "Pa-pa". "No mommy they have Pa-pa. Why can't he come with us? I need to stay with my Pa-pa! We have to go with Pa-pa." I could feel Charlie as my father in this lifetime outside the building they put us in to gas us. I could hear him screaming. I heard him trying to get in to us. Peggy who I only know by the name mom in this lifetime was holding on to me tight as she could trying to cover my head so I couldn't hear the firing of the squad that took out my Pa-pa. In my memory she was holding me as the sprinklers of what I thought was rain came over us. I was crying and she was still and brave telling me that we would be with Pa-pa soon. I knew she was right. I thought I would see him coming in to save us from the soldiers. Instead it was a new lifetime she bought him to me to help me save us all from what I feel is the 5th Reich. That's a whole other book in itself.

Over the years Peggy has given me several peaks into things but only when the time is right. She doesn't want to get too ahead of our path in this lifetime.

Foreword

Most of us during our current lifetimes experience philosophical and/or real life situations and ask ourselves "did that really just happen" and/or "did I really just "see" - what I think that I just saw"? Unfortunately, we almost never reach out to enjoy and contemplate a possible/potential "spiritual moment". Then, as we later reflect on what we thought that we just saw – we wonder "was that "real" or was it my "imagination" or was it a "dream" or was I "hallucinating" for some strange reason.

Sadly - as we continue our daily life in the 3D world, we gradually dismiss the recent spiritual experience because we are busy moving on with our jobs, family lives and human responsibilities. Some of us may think, "I will return to that experience and analyze my thoughts because that really was a different experience" and yet we usually never finish the debate with ourselves as to what we saw and/or experienced at that point in time. Thus, we never allow ourselves to experience a truly spiritual moment eliminating the chance of raising our vibrations to experience a small part of the spiritual realm.

My question to all of us living on the planet Earth at this point in time, now May of 2022, is exactly as the spiritual questions posed in the widely acclaimed "baseball" movie "Field of Dreams" - "Do you hear "the voices" trying to come through to Ray Kinsella"? "If you build it - they will come"! Was this Ray Kinsella's over active imagination? And was "Go the distance" heard when Ray Kinsella was working in his farm field; was he overheated? Was Ray Kinsella truly crazy as Terrance Mann, played by James Earl Jones, suggested when they first met in the "Field of Dreams"?

So I ask you the reader of this book and citizen of the world - "Do you "SEE" the players practicing on the Field of Dreams"? Or do you feel that this movie is like an imaginary "fairy tale" for school children? The same dilemma confronted Annie, Ray Kinsella's wife in the movie, who saw the players clearly but then she was surprised to realize that her brother and his wife and her mother had "no-clue" about the players. They did not see the players and would not even consider that the players were practicing baseball on the Field of Dreams. Until, somehow and someway, toward the end of the movie, when everyone saw the players! They amazingly had been blessed and were now "enlightened"! They had experienced a true "Spiritual Epiphany"!

One of the major questions of our lives is the question we have as human beings - "Do we see the players and believe in our Spiritual Selves and the Spiritual realm" - or don't we? Were "Shoeless Joe Jackson" and the other old time ball players practicing on the ball field - or was this some kind of baseball fairy tale? Ray Kinsella, and his wife Annie and their daughter Karen saw the players without a doubt - and they couldn't understand why Annie's real-estate brother and his wife and even Annie's mother could not see the players?

Was the Corn Field in "The Field of Dreams" truly Heaven - where our true spiritual selves reside and never die - or is this a real good make believe movie for kids, families and baseball fans? Bert Lancaster, i.e. - "Doc Graham" and as a young baseball player was known as "Moonlight Graham", understood the difference between the 3D lives we are currently living and the Spiritual realm. When he crossed over the line that was drawn in the dirt near the baseball field and the bleachers, he knew that he was giving up his baseball dream in order to continue his life as a Doctor - thus saving Karen's life, who had fallen off of the bleachers while swallowing a part of a hot dog that was choking her.

Terrance Mann, i.e. James Earl Jones, understood that his life was about to come to an end and he was about to literally walk into the spiritual realm and into "Heaven" i.e. - the Corn Field for everlasting life! He was "ready to go" and was looking forward to the new discoveries ahead in the Spiritual realm. He never doubted the spiritual realm.

Amazingly, that is similar how my Spiritual evolution has evolved in this lifetime! Peggy's death and return to me is helping me finish my Spiritual Journey so that I can help and support others! I was Lucky when I grew up never doubting that there is a God/Creator and that we have Angels and Spirit Guides around us who we can call on for support! I believe that we are here to learn and that our True identity is of high vibration Spiritual Purity!

I was lucky to have a mom and dad that supported thinking that was not stuck in the lower vibrational tones of control that sometimes comes with our human existence. I had an earth-wife who like me and a lot of us, wrestled with the injustices of human existence. Higher vibrational thinking with the help of aligning our chakra systems and developing our Thymus our 3rd eye again will help humanity get back on track with our spiritual priorities!

So here is my story as I come out of the closet (sort of speak) with what I am sure will surprise many of my family and friends, YMCA, business and baseball colleagues. In order to live my true and authentic self and to be of service to our world as much as I can with the time I am being allotted to finish my current life, I am excited for this opportunity to be able to tell my story! My hope is that this book will help people be confident that God is real and that his messengers and helpers are ready to help and assist us!

I also hope to celebrate Peggy, not only as my College Fiancé', but to share her Awesome and Amazing Spiritual self, both during our college years and of course after her physical death of this current lifetime. I also hope to remind everyone of the immense horrors of DV and that someone like Peggy had to endure this fate is horrific.

Finally I hope to share the joy of baseball and life that doesn't have to be at the highest level of MLB. There is and has been a lot of great, entertaining Fun and Crazy baseball played on local and regional ball fields all over the USA for almost 200 years now! Most of the really Fun and Entertaining stories about baseball happen at the semi-pro, collegiate and amateur levels and are never captured as history. My baseball experiences with Peggy, during our College years, serve as a small example of the baseball experience in America that happens for thousands and thousands of really fine players and those associated with these teams and leagues.

Sincerely,
Charlie Lord, May of 2022

Chapter 1

The First Meeting of this Lifetime

In 1975 I was the Centerfielder for the Topeka Aces semi-pro team of the Northeast Kansas Stan Musial League. We were to play the Iola, Kansas team for a Saturday afternoon doubleheader in mid June. Most of the Iola players were Allen County Junior College players while most of our Topeka Aces team played for the Washburn University "Fighting Ichabods". Because the Allen County players were farm boys - and this Saturday was at the beginning of normally is called "Harvest Season" which means that the wheat crop was now deemed ready for harvest! Thus, the plans changed at the last moment and our afternoon doubleheader was changed and now scheduled for a Saturday evening doubleheader!

I was disappointed with this news not only because we had just arrived in Iola and were ready to play; but also because 3 big time Major League Baseball scouts were ready to watch us play! That evening the 3 scouts planned on attending the Lawrence (made up of mostly Kansas University players) game against the Kansas City Raiders. One of the 3 scouts - Tom Greenwade, who had signed Mickey Mantle, Bobby Murcer and Topeka's Lee and Jim Dodson. Lee was the GM of our Topeka Aces "semi-pro" team and normally also was the Manager. Lee's real job was the Dean of Students at Washburn University. Lee and his wife Kay were in Europe for the summer of 1975. Lee was like a 2nd father to me as I am most of our player would hang out at the Dodson house during our high school and college years! Lee introduced me to Tom Greenwade as he watched several of our games in 1970, 1971 and 1972. Mr Greenwade was looking at Lee's sons and good friends of mine, Jim and Dick Dodson who were both pitchers and power hitting first baseman. I also received attention from Mr Greenwade who once told me that I ran twice as fast (unconsciously I guess) when I played Centerfield compared to my departure from home (meaning my time from home to first base was below standard - which was partly because of my speed and partly because of trying to get uncoiled after my swing) plate after I hit the ball. Unfortunately, despite my League leading 395 batting average of 1975, my speed from home to first base was still unacceptable for playing professional baseball.

Our interim Manager in 1975 was Leonard Worthington, who arranged for the Topeka Aces players to "hang-out" at the Iola Managers house that Saturday afternoon as we were treated to fun hospitality and the NBC Game of the Week between the New York Yankees and the Boston Red Sox! One of the interested fans who decided to stay and hang out with us was an attractive young lass from the area who was attending Washburn University, and in fact, would be a Cheerleader beginning in the fall of 1975. When Peggy Chamberlain and My eyes met, I guess that you could say that it was Love at first sight - even though I could hardly utter a sentence that made any sense that hot summer day. Peggy was a beautiful brunet with big brown eyes and sensational char-broiled legs that looked as though she just came out of a deep fry cooker!

The great news was that after struggling to say anything that made any sense - I somehow regrouped enough to make a decent impression with Peggy and as luck would have it, I had one of my best doubleheader's ever!! (I was able to hit 2 Homeruns while driving in 10 runs) It was also a good evening for our Topeka Aces as we won a doubleheader which made me very happy, despite the fact that no scouts were in attendance. Actually, now that I think about it, the main "scout" who was in attendance was the beautiful, sweet, attractive and smart Ms Peggy Chamberlain. Peggy would achieve her Bachelor of Business Administration Degree from Washburn University in 1978 as I would achieve my Bachelor of Education Degree from Washburn also in 1978. Suffice to say that Peggy's GPA was considerably higher than mine but at the time - my batting average was higher than just about anyone who had ever played at Washburn University, including major leaguers Dave's Lopes, Jerry Robertson and Steve Simpson. In fact, no other student who ever attended Washburn University, has ever hit as many as 4 Homeruns in one day as I did on May 4, 1976 at Baldwin, Kansas against Baker University. I'll take my baseball record over anyone's GPA any day of the week - with the possible exception of "my" Margaret "Peggy" Chamberlain.

I begin here with this background as the setting for how our story begins and I wish that I could say that Peggy and I were married, had a family with a bunch of kids - but sadly I cannot. In fact, despite the fun and spirited times we shared together at Washburn University, we were only able to enjoy each other for a little more than 2 years in the mid 1970's. Peggy's focus on her studies and cheerleading along with helping her friends and family that allowed for us to get together only occasionally. I likewise was so focused on baseball and preparing myself for professional baseball because I was absolutely sure that I was going to play for the New York Yankees (no matter what the baseball scouts were saying). And if I am not able to play Centerfield like my 2 Yankee super-star heroes Mickey Mantle and Bobby Murcer, I will be happy to play left or right field in Yankee Stadium. Because of these reasons, Peggy and I were only able to "get together" once or twice a month. And because we were both a bit shy, and even hesitant of being seen in public and just wanted to enjoy each other; hardly anyone new about our dates and "get togethers". Yet, when we were together we hit it off magically, and were so much alike that falling in Love was really easy - as if we had been together before. Peggy definitely had a strong aura around her many times as well as strong intuitive and even psychic abilities. I will never forget a birthday doubleheader I had in 1977 when we played Fort Hays State on Saturday and Benedictine College on Sunday. I went 9 for 12 with 4 Walks in those 4 games. Peggy could not attend because of family issues but when I called her to tell her what had happened she already knew and in turn repeated to me with great detail what had happened! I was dumbfounded by her remarks. While I sometimes had intuition when I was young with my mom and at various times in my life, my intuitive thought and psychic ability seemed to be "hit and miss". The fun thing that resulted was that Peggy and I did not have to talk about Love and Marriage - we just felt it and absorbed it and knew it for each other! It really was like we had known each other before - maybe many times before!

How and Why were we not only NOT married, and did NOT have kids, but somehow lost each other for almost exactly 40 years, is even amazing to me. 40

years - forty long years - and it was 45 years after we first met on that summer day in Iola, Kansas in 1975. The only thing that is more amazing to me is that on the evening of April 28, 2020 - during a violent spring Kansas thunder and lightning storm in Wichita - Peggy came back to me with the power of a locomotive! I went almost 40 years - from September of 1978 until August of 2018 pushing the memories of her back into the recesses of my mind because of the mental and psychological pain that it caused me thinking a thought about Peggy Chamberlain. It was at Lawrence/Dumont Stadium in Wichita; in its last baseball season at the National semi-pro baseball tournament; that Peggy came back into my mind and consciousness with accelerated frequency for the first time since 1978. I remembered Peggy sitting in the higher seats behind the batter at Lawrence-Dumont Stadium looking "as pretty as a picture" as I played Centerfield for the Topeka Aces in 1975. Now in 2018, as a volunteer for the National Semi-Pro Tournament, in the last year of the great old Lawrence-Dumont Stadium, remembering the times of my youth.

Playing for the Topeka Aces with all of the memories of my teammates and coaches, our opponents and games and including most of all, my beautiful Peggy! During this volunteer stint in August of 2018 almost out of nowhere, memories of Peggy came rushing back into my mind several at a time, almost as if someone had opened the floodgates of my mind. In the previous 40+ years I suddenly would think of Peggy in the oddest places such as on top of the pitchers mound in LittleRock, Arkansas, or taking a chess class in Plainview, Texas, or giving an important board of directors speech for one of my YMCA's or at a funeral. The pain and agony of the thought of Not having Peggy with me in this life was excruciating as I would push her back further and further into the back of my mind. How in the world, could it be that for 40 years, after we seemed to hit it off so well in the mid 1970's that I in essence lost her? And when I did think of her why would I continually push the thoughts of her back into the recesses of my mind? The "Miracle" is that I was about to become aware of - was that we were in essence "spiritual buds" of the same cloth - and have been for many previous lifetimes!

For the next 2 years after August of 2018 and 2019 and early in 2020 I began thinking of Peggy more and more on a regular basis without pushing thoughts of her back into the recesses of my mind! I was beginning to sense that someone was helping me deal with this personal hurt of my mind, body and spirit. I was about to find out that it was Peggy herself, now on the other side, along with our angels, spirit guides and family who were helping me unpack and free up my mind. This all helped clear my mind so that on the evening of April 28, 2020 when, as I mentioned, she came through in my mind so powerfully, that it was like receiving high definition messages, pictures and telepathic communication! Suddenly I began realizing and celebrating Peggy's presence in and around me with amazingly strong karma! It was thrilling to be a part of this influx of Peggy and this positive energy! Peggy's messages began with colors such as beige, pink, amber, blue and purple. The incredible feeling is that I knew that it was Peggy sending me these messages. The messages began with the color beige and she kept showing me that color in my mind for 4-5 days. Then I got the idea that it might be possible that colors stood for some kind of meaning and sure enough I was correct! Beige stands for energy and strength - the kind that is strong, dependable and can be trusted! Beige is linked to intellectual abilities, wisdom, ideas and knowledge! Holy Cow - this is an amazing education for me and Peggy knows that I know hardly anything about the art world, so what a great way to communicate with me!

About a week after April 28th, Peggy is riding on the passenger side of my Toyota 4 Runner wearing a Pink shirt with a dark skirt! She looks sharp, happy and in charge! She also looks focused, confident yet at ease and enjoying coming through to me. Her messages are not unlike the messages that came through "Ray Kansella" in the Field of Dreams! Remember "if you build it they will come" and "go the distance" from the Field of Dreams. Well I absolutely was receiving these kind of messages from Peggy, in the first 2 months after April 28th as in high definition - both in color and in audio! Next I was shown the Pink shirt that Peggy was wearing and after about 10 minutes she then added white pearls around her neck. The color Pink represents compassion, nurturing and Love. Bingo - this is the Peggy without a doubt that I knew in College in the mid 1970's. It relates to unconditional Love and compassion and the giving and receiving of nurturing Love! The Peggy that I knew in the 1970's and that I would learn to Love again in the next few months, is all of these qualities and more! Honesty, Caring, Respect and Responsibility with and including an immense nurturing Love that somehow pierced through my soul. In short a wonderful passionate and spiritual person whose persona seemed to be intuitive without a lot of negative vibrations and ego. Peggy really seems to have a very mature inner spiritual nature that I definitely noticed and was just beginning to understand myself.

But before we get into the day by day diary, I would like to flashback to 3 experiences that I had with Peggy during our college days at Washburn University and/or during the Topeka Aces summer baseball season at a time in the mid 1970's when we were roughly 20 and 21 years of age.

Meeting my unexpected True Love for the 1st time in of all places, Iola, Kansas! Yes despite my disappointment of not playing an afternoon doubleheader in front of 3 big name Major League Baseball scouts - It turned out to be a wonderful summer June day in 1975 in Iola, Kansas. Because the doubleheader was switched from afternoon to evening, the players, coaches and fans had time talk and visit. There were at various times 12-25 players and coaches and fans in a relatively large living room at the Iola baseball manager's house. We were just hanging out and passing time until 6:30 or so when it would be time to get to the baseball field to get ready for the game. It was a bit odd - but on this particular day lovely Peggy Chamberlain was the only young college age female in the group and for a while must have felt as though she was "bait in the middle of alligators" as one of our coaches not so tactfully put it. I actually felt sorry for Peggy as she was sure beautiful, shy and a little bewildered in this environment in and around baseball fanatics. That is when I began to break through a bit with Peggy visiting with her about Washburn and her major and favorite professors etc. Peggy seemed to appreciate my efforts to make her a part of the group as we players talked and ragged on each other in almost another language. We also had one eye on the Yankee vs Red Sox game on TV. 2 things stood out to me about Peggy: 1) how soft Peggy's demeanor was and how respectful and humble she was as she even offered to pick up and help clean up after we ordered hamburgers, fries and cokes for everyone. And 2) how focused she was on getting her very impressive Business Administration degree from Washburn's extremely highly rated school of business. The Washburn school of business was rated with Harvard and Yale as the top business schools in the country! When I then interjected that I received a "C" in basic math and even a "B" in Baseball Coaching Class, she tried not to laugh - which made holding it together worse, she couldn't help but to bust out laughing! I of course took no offense and was actually proud of myself for conversing with her and making her laugh. I could tell that she felt bad about laughing and she later pated my hand saying something like "I know that you can do better". I then told Peggy what my parents told me recently about my elementary school teachers who had told my parents that "he looks like he is paying attention", as they referred to my "C" student status. Peggy busted out laughing again and I knew that at the very least that I had made a decent impression and had new friend. During the doubleheader now in the evening, I noticed that up in the stands Peggy was visiting with quite a few people from the Iola area. I was sure happy to have a cheerleader rooting for me and it wasn't surprising I guess, that I was inspired to hit 2 Homeruns and drive in 10 runs in our doubleheader win! Darn - if only those 3 high profile scouts had been there? My new scout, a beautiful female, more than made up for it!

Chapter 2

Meet me at the Library

"Meet me at the Library"! Peggy and I really connected as being extremely attracted to each other by playing the "radar love" and/or "googlieye" game at Washburn University basketball games in the winter of 1975-1976 and again in the winter of 1976-1977. I just felt that Peggy was the cutest cheerleader ever! Peggy and would find each other's eyes and then I just couldn't take my eyes off of her - for the rest of the game. Our eyes met often during each game and we developed a "game within the game" where even if the ball and basketball action on the court went to the other end - I was not supposed to take my eyes off of her. If I would accidentally watch the game and the play at the other end of the court from where Peggy was cheerleading; she would put her hands on her hips as if she was very upset with me. A few times Peggy, would even fake a sad look on her face! The first time that Peggy made the sad look I forgot where I was and busted out laughing so loud that I was heard above the crowd noise.

With all of this I was still having trouble corralling Peggy for a date as she was actually very elusive. I think part of her elusive behavior was her dedication to her studies as well as Cheerleading and Alfa Gamma Theta activities. Sadly, there was also a bit of a mysterious feeling that she was forlorn to experience some sort of negative behavior or happening in her life. I could not put my finger on it but at times when we were together, once in a while, this feeling of "doom and gloom" would completely take me by surprise because she was normally so nice, positive and supportive. I sometimes wonder if a person kind of knows something tragic may happen to them even long before it actually happens? (I had the same intuitive feeling with my YMCA hero and mentor Jerry Robertson who died in a tragic car accident near Lebo, Kansas in 1995. Jerry would do some things that made me feel as though he knew something in his future could be a tragic event). I actually felt that because of this "doom and gloom" feeling that Peggy was a bit hesitant about going out publicly sometimes even for a date with me.

At any rate I finally chased Peggy down after a basketball game and asked her if she would like to go out for a Coke or a beer somewhere? Peggy answered that she was already going to the "Library" and said to come meet her there! So not wanting to be "uncool" I assumed that Peggy meant the new sports bar in Lawrence where a lot of Kansas University students and fans were going. "The Library" was the hot new party place in Lawrence. I told Peggy that I will get my car and see her in about 20 minutes thinking that "The Library" was about a 20 minute drive from Topeka to Lawrence. Peggy gave me kind of a funny look as I went to get my car and drive over to "the Library" in Lawrence. (note - as I was visiting with Peggy we were about 250 feet from the Washburn University Library on campus).

After driving over to Lawrence I finally find where "the Library" is but soon realized that hardly anyone was in the sports bar on this cold January evening. After waiting 15 minutes it finally hit me that Peggy might have meant that she was actually going to study at the Washburn Library on campus. Holy Cow "did I misread this one" I was thinking to myself as I drove back over to the Washburn campus. Luckily I got to the Washburn University Library a few minutes before it closed at 10:45ish and there was Peggy studying at a table by herself, as "pretty as a picture". I rushed over to her and sat down and apologized and tried to explain my thinking and my misunderstanding. Peggy just smiled and reached over for one of her pencils which happened to have an eraser on the top that looked like a hammer. She then proceeded to bong me on top of my head a few times! We both busted out laughing as did the tables around us! The Librarian then came over, who was a student-intern not much older than we were, and asked us to be quiet with everyone studying. I asked the Librarian "what is everyone doing in here anyway - especially after a basketball game"? Peggy then stated to me matter of factly that it is called "studying"! To which I replied "why would anyone want to do that after a basketball game"? At which time the Librarian borrowed Peggy's pencil with the hammer-eraser on the top and proceeded to bang my head several times as Peggy had just done. The entire place cracked up as people began to leave with closing time nearing.

Peggy and I met several times in the Washburn University and/or the Topeka Public Library for "study" dates as I had to be careful not to get to playful or to funny - not only so that she could study but so that everyone else could also. But every so often a funny scene re-occurred as the student-intern librarian took a liking to Peggy and I. These were the young and innocent days of 2 kids growing up fast and falling in Love and not knowing what our place in the world will be - but hopefully, whatever it will be, Peggy and I will be together - for sure! These kind of funny interactions are priceless and since neither one of us had a lot of money, (what college kids do?) these kind of get togethers were more or less our dates. And neither one of us minded a bit. We were with each other, and we knew most of our friends at the library studying, and the student librarian was a lot of fun!

On another occasion I came to meet Peggy at the Washburn University Library as she was in her usual place to study. Our favorite student-intern Librarian was in a good mood as Peggy seemed to be in an extremely playful mood also! Of course, probably because of their good moods, I created disturbances by talking too loud with a boisterous with my joyous attitude. I was really playing well for the Washburn baseball team and we had a good shot at getting in the NAIA District 10 playoffs in 1976. So the Librarian asked me to go upstairs for a while and let Peggy and the students around us tend to their studying. The librarian suggested that I look for baseball magazines and I told her about the Life Magazine with Elizabeth Taylor and Richard Burton on the cover. The Librarian asked what does studying or baseball have to do with Richard Burton and Elizabeth Taylor? I told the Librarian about the advertisement for Post Cereals in that Life Magazine ie "March of 1962". The Post Cereal add has Roger Maris and Mickey Mantle baseball cards attached to the Life Magazine and "here in 1976", these 2 baseball cards were already worth thousands! I asked the Librarian if she thought that it would be stealing if I tore out the Mantle and Maris cards that were attached to the Post Cereal add? As the Librarian thought for a moment Peggy is looking at me incredulously probably wondering what kind of nut that she is beginning to fall in love with? The Librarian looks at me and says "I'll tell you what? My dad just loves Roger Maris and you love Mickey Mantle so give me the Maris card and we both win"! After the Librarian mentioned that compromise - Peggy takes her pencil with the rubber hammer eraser at the top and boings both the librarian and myself on the head - to the laughter of the entire library population that evening!

Our first "real date"! After a while I was determined to have a "real date" with Peggy and so I suggest Godfathers Pizza on 29th Street! I told Peggy "how much more of a fun date can you have than Godfathers Pizza - and YOU get to go out with a "C" student who can't dance and I'll pick you up driving my Luxurious Lime-Green Pinto that doesn't have a radio"! I mentioned all of this partly because I was becoming a bit of a local celebrity, and I did not want Peggy to feel uncomfortable with whatever my new local celebrity status entailed. As I mentioned we were both shy but fairly secure and fairly confident even though at times we both retreated-away into our introvert tendencies. Thus as we "prepared" for our big Pizza date, I would remind Peggy that she was lucky to be going out with - not only a "C" student and a bad dancer, but would get to ride in my beautiful - lime green - Ford Pinto that didn't even have a radio in the dash! How much more class and fun can you have than that? I was having a hard time reading her reaction to my repeated statement but she said that she was looking forward to our big Pizza date. So the big day finally arrived and I was nervous all day. Kind of a mix between excitement yet trepidation with fearful thinking like "what if she doesn't like me or what if this play on words comes back to haunt me"? As it turns out she slyly has a trick up her sleeve that seemed totally out of character but made this incident so funny and memorable. Finally the time had come as I pulled up to guess what - the Washburn Library to pick her up - and as I opened the passenger door for her - I reminded her of the status that she was going to have tonight! A beautiful cheerleader going out with a "great" student and getting picked up in a Lime Green Ford Pinto - with no radio! Well, as I mentioned Peggy got me real good on this one as I was almost horrified at what happened next. As she was about to get into my car Peggy squealed a squill that I had never even come close to hearing from her. And she yelled out "I'm sorry Charlie (have you ever heard that line before?) but I can't take all of this anymore! A "C" Student, an ugly Lime Green Car with no radio, and now I discover a no cloth seat and no rubber mats for my feet. I'm sorry - I have to go! Peggy ran back over to the Theta House bellowing out some kind of noises. I sat there totally numb, dumbfounded and stunned. I thought to myself "Holy Toledo - was I imagining this"? I had never seen her like this before? This looks as though it is a colossal and extremely embarrassing melt down. So I drive very sheepishly and slowly over to the Theta House thinking that surely this was some kind of prank? Or was it? Did I really not know her well after-all? What should I do? I thought about driving off mad - but what good would that do? It just didn't seem like her? So after about 10 minutes or so - which seemed more like 10 hours - I began to get out of my Pinto and gingerly walk up to the Theta House door - but I just couldn't do it. So I slinked back into my Pinto and after a few more minutes, sadly started the car up - and began to back up - when all of a sudden - Peggy and 2 of her friends come running out of the Theta House laughing unabashedly at the joke that she just played on me! Man was I relieved and she really had me going! I was almost sickly and I am sure that I looked that way - so she game a big hug and smooch on the cheek! Still semi-stunned and still almost shaking I offered to take her 2 friends with us but they declined - so we made sure they got some Pizza when we returned! Jeez that was a good one Peggy! BTW - we had a great time at Godfathers Pizza and that thick Pizza was hard to eat too much so Peggy had plenty for her Theta friends! When we sat down at Godfathers a neighbor of mine on West 19th Street was having a birthday party for one of his 2 kids and took pictures of Peggy and me. In fact I used his camera to take a picture of Peggy and she took one of me (see the pictures). The one of me still survives but I lost the one of her and especially the one of us in one of my many YMCA relocations - darn it. When I drove Peggy back to Theta house we first stopped at the Dairy Queen for an ice creme cone! She got one with sprinkle things all over it! Then I walked her up to the door of the Theta House and she gave me a wonderful good night kiss! One that curled my toes for about 20 days! And how I could still taste some of the sprinkle things from the ice creme cone! Wow - It was great to be 21 and in college and playing baseball and dating Peggy! How can anything ever get better than this?

Baseball, Baseball and more Baseball

Chapter 3

College Baseball and the Minor Leagues with Peggy

In the Summer of 1976 and in 1977 and Spring of 1978 I ramped up my baseball training regime to maximum levels. Because of this, and with Peggy really hitting the books hard so that she could graduate in May of 1978, we actually lost track of each other a few times even though she always knew that she could probably find me at the ballpark. Back in 1976, during my Junior year at Washburn, scouts began to finally show an interest in my baseball abilities. It was the spring of 1976 and I was having a very solid Junior season when we went to Baldwin to play Baker University on May 4th. This was to be our next to last doubleheader of the year. Unfortunately we just missed the playoffs again losing to Emporia State 8-7 at Emporia on April 30th. We had beaten Emporia State 2 out of the first 3 games and if we beat them on April 30th we knock them out of the playoff hunt and we take their place. If we lose we knock ourselves out of the playoff race. A large crowd gathered at Emporia including Peggy and about 5 friends and I came through with a Double and a Triple to account for 5 RBI's. I was on 3rd base in the top of the last inning with a runner on first when our batter was called out on a bang-bang double play. It was a heartbreaking loss even though we had several MLB scouts in attendance watching. I looked up and caught a brief glimpse of Peggy after the game with a tear in hear eye. She was so sweet and so loyal and exuded so much Love.

The same scouts were at Baldwin on May 4th and unfortunately in my 1st at bat I hit a towering fly ball against the wind, that the Baker University left fielder caught with his back to the wall for a fly out. As the 1st game of the doubleheader continued we noticed that the wind began turning around and in my 3rd at bat I was looking for a fastball "up and in" meaning to the inside part of the plate. I got it and drove it hard on a line drive down the line for a Home run! This is a pitch I did not usually hit well but looking for this type of pitch can sometimes make all of the difference in the world.

In my first at bat of the second game I got a fastball that began inside and faded away to the outside part of the plate from a tough left handed pitcher. Fortunately I tracked it well and got all of it with my 35" - 34 ounce Johnny Callison Louisville

Slugger! The ball went almost 500 feet to dead center field - al be it with the help of the spring wind that had now turned all the way around helping the batters. Note - I still used a wood bat but the rest of my teammates had switched over to an aluminum Louisville slugger bat. The aluminum bat had a rubber end and a rubber grip and the ball came off the bat very close to a wood bat. The advantage was playing sometimes chilly and cold spring weather, the aluminum bat didn't sting as much and was not in danger of breaking. In the next year the Easton bat company introduced a bat that I thought was in danger of injuring a pitcher and even an infielder because the ball came off the bat so much faster. This was the predecessor to the "Gorilla bats" used in college baseball in the 1980's and 1990's.

With 2 Home runs in 2 at bats our 3rd base coach, Lonnie Krueger, suggested that I look for an off speed pitch - which I did, and sent it out over the left field fence for my 3rd Home run of the day! In my next at bat I was not sure what to expect so after a pitch buzzed me inside in an attempt to back me off of the plate, I looked for a breaking pitch and got one sending it out over the trees in right-center field! With 4 Home runs on the day I Doubled in my last at bat short hoping the right-center field fence. And "dog gone it" I was on deck when we made the third out in the last inning. After this game I received inquiries from 13 different Major League teams! With the MLB Draft a month away I felt sure that I would be drafted around the 15th round! But unfortunately disaster struck the very next day on the Washburn University baseball field as we had an informal workout preparing for our final doubleheader of the season at St Joseph to face William Jewel College. In the informal workout one of my cleats got stuck in a crevasse locking my left shoe/foot while the rest of my body moved in the opposite direction. My left knee collapsed suddenly leaving me immobile and wincing in pain. The knee swelled up to the size of a volleyball and I knew that I would not be able to play the next day in St Joesph - which was a favorite ballpark of mine. It was an old Minor League ballpark where I pitched my best game ever for the Topeka Aces in 1970. Sadly - that night Peggy wanted to take me out to celebrate my 4 Home run day - and my bad knee injury prevented us from doing that. She came over to the house and we shared a Coke and talked about getting together during the summer season as I was determined to somehow get myself well enough to play for the Topeka Aces in the summer of 1976. I needed to recover so that the Major League Baseball scouts would not "get wind" of my knee injury because this would be devastating for my draft chances in the Major League Draft that always happens around June 12-13.

The summer of 1976 was incredibly disappointing despite the fact that I was able to get my knee in shape enough to bat 353 with 6 Home runs for the Topeka Aces of which I was named player/manager despite still having 1 year of College Baseball eligibility left at Washburn. Unfortunately, the MLB scouts sniffed out my knee injury and by-passed me altogether in the draft. The extremely unfortunate timing of my knee injury at a time when I finally really had the MLB scouts interest was heartbreaking. Peggy attempted to make me feel better as we went out after a couple of Topeka Aces games and happily had what amounted to "kiss-a-thorns" in my "beautiful" Lime-Green Pinto! I think that she was attempting to make me feel better and she sure did with her quiet, supportive and caring attitude - not to mention her wonderful kisses! Peggy's schedule was really getting busy with school, and work and with an internship. She informed me that she would not be returning as a Cheerleader for Washburn in the fall. That information saddened me quite a bit as it meant an end to our innocent "googleye" game at Washburn University basketball games. After our 2 get togethers during the summer of 1976 sadly Peggy and I hardly saw each other in person ever in 1976. If we did I do not remember it. She was working so hard to work and graduate and I was now not only working hard to get ready for my Senior baseball season at Washburn University and still holding on to my professional baseball dreams that were still lingering - and I was having to take care and massage my knee injury. At this time there was no easy remedy for knee injuries as the arthroscopic knee surgery had not yet made its medical surgery appearance. Thus knee surgery meant ripping the knee open completely and I had not seen any evidence that it was all of that successful. My Topeka surgeon suggested immediate knee surgery but I balked and went into my senior season ready to play on an injured left knee.

In the spring of 1977 I had not come to grips with my knee nor the fact that Peggy and I would not see much of each other in 1977 either. I was still intending to play my senior baseball season and still was intent of pursuing Peggy "when the time was right" even though I didn't really realize that I had actually already lost track of her - again. I was getting unprecedented publicity for Washburn University Baseball and this helped negate in my mind my lack of hustle to pursue Peggy. My publicity also helped disguise my bad knee but somehow/someway - I had an outstanding senior season at Washburn batting 412 with 8 Home runs! The MLB scouts were paying attention again and pointed to the fact that in my 111 plate appearances for the 1977 season I walked an amazing 26 times and only struck out only 2 times. Both of those figures got me many compliments from scouts and professional baseball organizations alike. Those last 2 stats peaked the scouts interest as I received letters from Toronto, Montreal, Seattle and several Independent Class A level Minor League teams. MLB was beginning to use the success of the Independent teams for players like me who may have had injury challenges, or for sports stars whose baseball playing time was limited for baseball. With much of the PR and focus on me and the fact that we finally made the NAIA baseball playoffs for the first time was exciting for all of us! Sadly missing in my joy most of the spring of 1977 was Peggy. I really expected her to turn up at a game or 2 and what little time that I had - I could not find her anywhere.

Then on my birthday weekend April 2nd and 3rd Peggy showed up for a Saturday doubleheader with Benedictine School and on Sunday for Fort Hays State. I had a terrific weekend going 9-12 with 4 Walks as we won all 4 games! Peggy was my good luck charm again! After the Sunday game we went out to a new pizza place and to a drive in movies at the Chief drive in. What a birthday present that was! We were both so busy the time just flew by as I had a tryout with Toronto in June and almost made it but they wanted me to get knee surgery - which I did in October. Peggy told me that I might not see her for a while because of her heavy school and work schedule so we left it up to her to arrange free time for our dates.

So in the fall of 1977 with no Peggy in sight, I continued to rehab my knee after my October 23rd operation. During the Christmas holidays Peggy called and I managed to get her to go to the Big 8 basketball tournament in Kansas City. She was horrified when I told her that I had my knee surgery without her and she broke down crying as I could tell that she was feeling the pressure of coming down the home stretch before graduation at Washburn. She was fighting for good grades, and attempting to do well with an intern-type job and wished that she and I had more time together.

In the spring of 1978 I was the last one cut for a Minor League team in Alexandria, Virginia. My knee was not 100% yet but I was invited to try out for a Minor League team in Victoria BC, Canada in May of 1978. The Class A Northwest League was adding 3 Independent teams to the league for players like myself. I hit the jackpot even though I was competing against 100 college players, who were all recommended by MLB scouts, for 25 roster spots. The scout who helped me was former Kansas City Athletics 3rd baseman, Ed. Charles. Mr Charles was now a scout for the New York Mets and had seen me play many times. The Victoria minor league tryouts went on for 11 days! Many of the days included 2 and 3 workouts! Finally - on June 12th - it was announced that I made the last cut and was a member of the Victoria Mussels of the Class A Northwest Minor League! Wow - I did it - I made a Minor League team!!! I was very honored as the team could have been made up by any 25 of the 100 players elected to tryout. In fact this tryout camp is my #1 personal baseball highlight for me and to think that all I just went through with my knee injury makes it all worthwhile!

At highlight of my #1 overall baseball thrill was - The extremely difficult "big boy" drill - was that I had 20 Strikes to do damage against several pitchers in camp who were also attempting to make the team. If I swung and missed at a ball it reduced my available strikes by 1. If I swung and missed or hit a foul ball, it counted against me. All of the pitchers that I faced could really throw hard and most had good control and knew where it was going and how to pitch. A few did not and if the pitch was a ball it worked against the pitcher. Because I was really physically, mentally and emotionally ready (except for missing Peggy - but I had not given up on her showing up yet) and had the experience of a couple of other tryout camps, with Minor League teams - I was really ready! I was extremely confident at bat and I was hitting all pitches with verve in practices.

Alleluia - what a performance if I may say so myself! Of my 20 strike pitches I belted an amazing 12 out of sight for Home runs! Everyone was amazed (as was I also to be quite honest). The next best hitter hit only 3 Home-runs in that "big-boy" drill. I not only had not ever seen these pitchers before but had not ever been to this baseball field before in Victoria, British Columbia, Canada. In the Victoria coaches evaluation rating system - 18 of my "strikes" would have gone for base hits! The next best player had 8. Needless to say that I was overjoyed and could not wait to get the 1978 Northwest League season underway! I was excited and absolutely could not wait! I only wish that I could have had Peggy to share these moments with. In fact a friend told me that Peggy was going to attend Kansas University in the fall of 1978 for some graduate hours. I was determined to go find her after this season and pursue her when I would get back from my Minor League season. I did not let myself think of it too much but when I did I was really mad at myself for not communicating with her and for loosing track of her.

In the summer of 1978 my Minor League Baseball season at Victoria was bitter-sweet. Yes I was elated to finally be playing Minor League baseball! And when I did play - I played really well - batting in the prestigious 4th spot in the batting order. I received great feedback from my teammates, coaches, opponents and scouts alike. The sad reality was however, that I was not able to stabilize my left knee enough to gain consistent playing time. It was swelling up all of the time even after my operation in the fall of 1977. Back in 1978 there, unfortunately, was no "Advil" that could help stop and prevent swelling and in those days there was no arthroscopic surgery yet. As I mentioned earlier, by ripping moon my knee open for surgery, made the recovery and rehabilitation extremely difficult. But I was still very determined to give Professional Baseball a chance even though, as my teammates kidded me, that I had more actual procedures to "drain blood and fluid out of my knee" than official Minor League at bats. A Knee draining was excruciatingly painful. After a knee draining I would play for 3-4 days and feel good but then gradually my knee would begin filling up with blood again. Still as I mentioned I had my moments and it was Pete Ward, scout for the Yankees who really liked my swing! Every time I saw Pete we talked a lot about batting. He loved my stance and my swing and really took an interest in me! (Pete Ward was the 1963 Rookie of the year for the American League when he played for the Chicago White Sox).

Not knowing exactly where Peggy was and not knowing how to contact her was a very difficult emotion and sad reality for me as I would have loved for her to share even a few minor league moments with me. As I mentioned she could be elusive and even in the late 1970's it could be difficult to find people - even if it was my "dream-girl". The Class A Northwest League had several wonderful ballparks with great ambiance like Eugene, Oregon; Bellingham, Washington and Grays Harbor, Washington. Even Medford and Bend, Oregon were fun ballparks and cities to play in. Because my knee troubles lead to groin and hamstring problems my season did not begin until July 13 when we were playing at Eugene. (I had a couple more unexpected injuries as I tried to get ready for the season after I made the team). A beautiful minor league ballpark with big high walls and reminded me of My hometown And Topeka's Community ballpark where "my" 1961 Topeka Reds played as the 3-I League Class B minor league champions. (Back in those days Minor League Baseball had several classifications - AAA, AA, A, B, C, D and Independent).

In my first game as the Catcher, at the Eugene Emeralds Ballpark (Eugene was the Class A Farm Club of the Cincinnati Reds) I went 2 for 4 and was excited to get my first minor league game in the books. My most memorable game was at Olympic Stadium, built in 1912, at Grays Harbor, Oregon. This is a game that "Saturday Night Live" production crew was beginning to film a segment called "what I did on my summer vacation"! Grays Harbor is Bill Murray's hometown and most people know that Bill Murray is a huge baseball fan. Bill was there with about 250 of the Saturday Night Live production crew team members. The production crew and the large crowd made it a noisy and fun atmosphere that evening. In fact, most of the production crew was sitting either right behind us, and even on the field with us as our dugout was on the first base side. In fact I was told that 3 people from Kansas had driven 30+ hours to get to tonight's game that I did not know about. They were sitting in the middle of the production crew for Saturday Night Live! The big crowd at ancient Olympic Stadium made it really fun in this old wooden ballpark! The Public address announcer had a distinct style also and it was fun to hear my name being announced for my time at bat! I was proud to bat in the clean-up spot again! I had learned that the clean-up man gets buzzed with the first pitch to him in a minor league ballgame. So this was about my straight 7th buzz job! I actually took it as a compliment even though I wanted to hit the next pitch right back at the pitcher - which happened a couple of times! I hit the ball beautifully in this game with 4 picturesque 300-350 foot line drives! Unfortunately 3 were line outs at the left fielder, centerfielder and right fielder! I did get a Double up the right-centerfield gap. Grays Harbor was an Independent team with mature and good pitching and it was a real challenge to play them and to hit off of their pitchers. In fact they won the Northwest League title that season. Still to hit 4 Line deep line drives off good pitchers and pitches - but was only 1 for 4, was a frustrating experience. Boy I really felt good at the plate and my bad left knee was behaving tonight.

After my 4th 300 foot line drive outs that was caught, I was ready to uncharacteristically swear and throw my helmet, something that I did not like to do and I know that "my" Peggy would not have approved of. So when I turned back to the dugout - I saw the big crowd and production crew looking right at me - with some sympathetic faces, so I just mumbled a few things to myself and trotted back to the dugout. As I entered the dugout I noticed someone up in the crowd sitting in the middle of the Saturday Night Live production crew. I looked back again and up at this crowd as something again caught my eye in that maize of faces that I took to be the movie set workers. Then suddenly - I realized who it was - OMG - there was a beautiful angel in the middle of that crowd and it was "my Peggy"!!! As you can imagine - I was absolutely incoherent for several minutes as I kept peaking up in the crowd I could see the tears streaming down her face too. She somehow made it to Grays Harbor, Oregon to see me play! What a wonderful blessing this was!

As it turned out a couple of Peggy's friends saw the Saturday Night Live "Promo" a few weeks ago about Bill Murray with the summer vacation theme - and they checked the Northwest League schedule and drove 32 hours way out to Oregon. They shared driving time and sleep time. The bummer was that they were heading right back in the car back to Kansas because of their busy schedules. Peggy and I only had time for a few hugs and kisses - in front of everyone mind you - but I didn't care. There were still a lot of people hanging around, along with the Saturday Night Live production crew, after the game. The production crew must have loved our hugging and kissing and gave us a funny ovation when we finished! I also got "high-fives" from my teammates when I got back into the team bus!

Then Peggy asked me who Pete Ward is? I told her that he is the Yankee scout who seems to at least have some interest in me. Peggy told me that Pete Ward was talking to someone about me for 10 minutes and that he really liked me! Pete was sitting in the seat in front of Peggy with a couple of other baseball scouts. In fact Peggy quoted Pete saying that he said "I think that we can teach that kid to get more of his hips and his big strong butt into the swing! If he had done that tonight - he would have hit 4 Homers"! To which my punch-drunk and tired Peggy butted into the conversation telling Pete Ward "that is my future husband and you are right - he does have a nice big rear end"! They told me that everyone around Peggy and her friends - cracked up - Saturday Night Production Crew and all! Our Victoria team was about to load the bus and Peggy and friends were driving back to Kansas. All the while when I was hugging and kissing Peggy - I was thinking "thank goodness that I didn't throw my helmet and cuss after that 4th at bat)!

As the season went on my knee got worse and I had to come home early. I thought that would be my last Minor League experience and as brief as it was - it was a gratifying one! My stats were not bad with a 364 average and the possibility of returning next year but I had a lot of things to think about before the summer of 1979 arrived. 1) to pursue Peggy 2) to begin to seriously look for a career outside of baseball 3) to heal and get healthy with the possibility of one more try at professional baseball.

My first connection and thought of making the YMCA a career came in October when I interviewed with the Salina YMCA for a Fitness Director position. I finished 2nd but gained valuable insight and information about the YMCA and how it operates. The Salina YMCA staff said that they liked me and would holler if and when another opening happens. I also had interviews with Park and Recreation Departments, but did not like the stern feeling that seemed to pervade. I also took Officers Training skills test with the US Air Force. I did receive an offer from the Kansas "Job Help" program with a position that helped people become employed. I almost took that job but had an offer in February, which coincidentally was about the same time that all of the bruises on my legs from last summer's minor league season finally disappeared, to play for the Salem Oregon Senators in the Class A Northwest Minor League. Salem wanted to play me at first base and outfield and told me to forget Catching - which sounded wonderful to me!

In the fall of 1978 I was determined to find and pursue Peggy Chamberlain in an effort to "court her" and hopefully marry her. When I got back from my Minor League season I TRIED and Tried and tried to find Peggy until frustrated one night I cried, and cried and cried. It was a horrible feeling. Lee Dodson, the Dean of Students tried to help me, some of Peggy's acquaintances and friends tried to help but Peggy was really elusive back in a day and time you could get lost if you wanted to. My brother John was a great example of that as we lost track of him, at the age of 26 in 1970, as he was finishing up graduate work with Harvard Divinity School. John was 10 years older than I was and he was an "A" student and 3 time

Central Intercollegiate Conference tennis champion in both Singles and Doubles! After graduating from Washburn University in 1966 John received a Rockefeller Fellowship Scholarship to Harvard Divinity School. When he finished up his work with a practicum in Greenwich Village in 1970, it was the last time we talked to him until 1995. Earlier in 1970 he came home to get his stuff and it was the last time we saw him for 50 years.

The Viet Nam War, the strife and turbulence of the 1960's and 1970's and the Timothy Leary experimental drug stuff was present in society but with John I think that it could have been a mental breakdown and or depression. Johns fiancé Enie Shinn, wanted to get married after High School and our dad, who was an awesome dad, showed his tough-love skills and refused to send John anymore money after he graduated from Harvard Divinity School. John got mad and got lost in society over the next decade and only 1 person, a friend named Pete Woodward, who was an Episcopal Priest, really knew where John was. Now, it was so sad to realize, that my Peggy, probably for very different reasons, was lost to me and I did not know how to find her.

Back in the 1978 society had television, radio, land line telephone and no other way to track a person down other than person to person word of mouth. I could not trace Peggy down and I am not sure that a private detective could have either - and unfortunately - I did not have the money to pay for a private detective or private investigator. If it were today we have the internet and other tech tools and hundreds of other resources. I am going to have to rely on prayer and word of mouth to help me find my Peggy. It is hard to believe that she came all the way to see me in Oregon in July and I cannot find her anywhere now in November. This reoccurring theme and plot is beginning to challenge my emotional wellbeing. I do not know if Peggy has other boyfriend(s) or if there are other issues or if she is just like me, attempting to find her career path first? I did know that she was very insightful and very spiritual with strong intuitive gifts even back then. And I also knew that there was something special between us - even more than Love on this earthly plane - it was as if we have been together many times before! We get along so well and I "feel" her often through our intuitive and 3rd eye feelings, but I would sure like to have her around more often.

By the spring of 1979 I was working on getting my resume out for business, sports and baseball opportunities. I was also preparing happily for another shot of Minor League Baseball as my body suddenly rebounded in February and I was feeling like an almost 25 year old should feel! My workouts for the Salem Senators focused on playing and learning more about the first base position. The Salem team said "no more catching" and I loved it. As an independent minor league team, Victoria and Salem have the talent to compete in the Northwest Minor League Baseball League, but they own and pay the players. An affiliated team signs a working agreement with a big league ball club who supplies and pays for the players. The idea is to develop enough players so that they can climb the Minor League baseball ladder from Class A to AA and then to AAA Minor League Baseball so that they can be ready for the Major Leagues. Annually there are between 1,500 - 2,500 Minor League baseball players of which 200 might sniff the Major Leagues competing with 700 other Major League Baseball players. When I consider the fact that the 2,500 Minor Leaguers come from 100,000 college and amateur players annually. The odds to reach Major League Baseball are really long. In 1980, the success of Independent Minor League teams created a growth of Independent Minor Leagues that have not been seen since the 1900's and 1930's. Cities and towns want to have a Minor League team and Independent Minor League Baseball was a good way to operate an affordable professional baseball team!

When I arrived at the Salem Senators tryout camp at the end of May 1979, I had to lose my position rather than gain it - as I had to do a year ago with the Victoria Mussels. Still with almost 100 invited players in camp I did not want to lose my status as the team's first baseman. The 10 day preseason camp, like last year in Victoria, had several days of 2 and 3 workouts. I did not hit with the same power that I did a year ago in Victoria but I did hit very well and played a promising enough first base! About 3 days before the season began I was named the opening day first baseman as our opener was at Eugene on June 19th. This is a big moment for me personally as I Love the importance of Opening Day and to be a starter really made me happy! Eugene always had a big crowd and expected a sellout crowd on Opening Day. A day before opening day it was announced that the Seattle Mariners had purchased my contract! I was not quite sure what this meant as I was called to a meeting with owners of the Salem Senators and representatives of the Seattle Mariners. (Seattle was an American League expansion team along with Toronto in 1977).

So I was wondering if I was going to sign a contract for more money? I wondered if I would be sent to another Minor League team in the Seattle Mariners farm system? I wondered if they had special plans for me? Well I quickly found out that it was a big to-do over nothing because nothing really happened. Now the Seattle Mariners owned me and my baseball rights even though I still was playing for the Salem Senators of the Class A Northwest Minor League. The Salem Senators are now classified as a "Coop" Minor League team which means some of its players are paid for by a Major League team. The Seattle Mariners did pay the Salem Senators for my contract and my rights. I am not sure what the Seattle Mariners paid for me but I really did not care as I was just trying to get ready for Opening Day on a Minor League Baseball team!

The week leading up to "Opening Day" we played 3 games against area Semi-Pro teams similar to my Topeka Aces team. We beat the local teams in all 3 games and I was getting red hot at bat and felt really good as my knee was feeling very good also. I was receiving congrats from all over such as Washburn University teammates and connections, Topeka and Kansas friends and press and family members. My only disappointment was Peggy and not knowing where she was and/or what she was doing? Interestingly enough however, once it was announced by the press and media in Topeka, I started receiving strong positive telepathic communications and feelings and I am sure that it was from Peggy. I think using our intuition and developing our thymus and 3rd eye spiritual skills a bit, we all receive messages from spirits and from other human beings from time to time. I was really wondering if Peggy might have passed away somehow as she was really coming in strong! Could Peggy be communicating with me as a live human being with a passionate love and gifts of telepathic communication?

This communication reminded me of the communication that my mother and I would often have when I was 2-5 years of age. I remember one period of time that I went several days without really saying anything to my mother because we knew what each other was doing all of the time. The communication that I was receiving before June 19, 1979 was significant but I did not really know how to handle it or how to deal with it yet.

Well the big day, June 19th 1979 has arrived as we prepared and entered Eugene Emeralds ball park! As I mentioned earlier, it was a real fun Minor League ballpark with awesome ambiance! During batting practice a grizzled Cincinnati Reds coach/scout that I met in February at the Reds tryout camp at Tampa, Florida hollered at me. "Hey pretty boy - it looks like you didn't learn a thing in February! You are to damn stubborn to learn anything and as blasted me and my batting stance. It was very unprofessional and unsettling barrage of insanity meant to do nothing more than to shake me up. The grizzled veteran scout did not like my Carl Yastrzemski like batting stance which was natural to me, as my hands were held high and I was away from the plate and deep in the box. The grizzled old coach continued to send negative remarks at me even intimating that I will never be able to swing quick enough to hit this pitcher that the Eugene Emeralds have pitching today. I was embarrassed for this grizzled old veteran who had also accused my friend, Jim Dodson, of stealing his Cincinnati Reds hat when we were at Tampa for that 3 day tryout camp back in February. The bombardment of insults continued for 2-3 minutes as our players were becoming uncomfortable for me and began yelling at the grizzled old coach for me - and this didn't stop for about 5 minutes of back and forth of yelling that was probably a way to release tension. I did not say a word but very much appreciated my teammates standing up for me!

Batting in the Opening Day lineup in the clean-up #4/position I was confident and ready to go as we were introduced with the Opening Day ceremonies. I had good intuition all week that something great was going to happen for me tonight! And then at the end of the week - I am sure that I felt Peggy's prayers and telepathic communication coming in strong for me. I was trying to capture the "Opening Day" moment for myself because this was really fun and something I had dreamed about for years. Playing Minor League Baseball-on Opening Day in the Northwest Minor League, before a big crowd, in a really cool ballpark! If only "my" Peggy were here. The pregame ceremonies were fun and hilarious with the Eugene owner flying in on a helicopter and landing on the pitchers mound with the game ball.

As I got ready to hit in the first inning I had the grizzled scouts words ringing in my ears loud and clear, but unfortunately, after striking out only 2 times my senior year in college - and only 2 times in my first minor league season last year, I struck out in my first at bat tonight, much to the satisfaction of the grizzled veteran with the Cincinnati Reds. He let me have it for the first 3 innings as I took my position at first base in innings 1, 2 and 3. Our Salem Senator first base coach, a gruff guy himself, told me that he was going to stuff a baseball down the "old goats" throat the next time he would go out to the coaches box!

My second time at bat came in the top of the 4th inning as we trailed Eugene 1-0. With a runner on first base and 1 out our Manager put the "hit and run play" on which meant that the runner on first base is going to run for second base and it was my job to protect him, by trying to hit the pitch, wherever it comes in. The batter really has to have great batting-skills as he has to get a piece of the ball to either get a base hit or to put the ball in play, which would normally advance the runner even if I made an out. At our Salem Senator practices I was the best Hit and Run batter on the team, meaning I had the best bat control and actually had several successful hit and run plays with Victoria last year. One other condition that our

Salem Manager wanted me to do when he put the "hit and run" play on when I batted, is that if the pitchers pitch came inside, he wanted me to turn on the pitch and attempt to blast it out of the park! Wow that is the first and only manager, I have ever known, who gave these kind of instructions for the "hit and run" play. Normally if the pitch came inside, the batter was to pull his hands in and try to hit the ball to the right side of the infield and to right field, so that the base runner on first could get to second base, and thus he would be in scoring position.

So here comes the pitch from the powerful Eugene Emerald pitcher at 95 mph I was told. Well, on a hit and run play, I began my swing a bit early as I wanted to make sure that I hit the ball somewhere and with this pitcher throwing very hard this was a big help to me! As the pitch came in I realized it was coming inside so I took the mighty swing that our Salem Senator Manager wanted me to take! Low and behold I really nailed it - as I actually saw the backward spin on the ball as it left the bat almost in high definition - and it was a real titanic blast, if I say so myself!! I heard the crack of the bat, the oohs and awes of the crowd as the ball sailed high and mightily over the big scoreboard! I found out later, the ball cleared the parking lot, for a blast of close to, if not more than, 500 feet! My teammates were so excited they lined up 1 by 1 along the 3rd base line, to give me "high-5's" and pats on the back! It was the most electric moment of my baseball career. A Mickey Mantle type clutch moment for sure! Then my teammates delighted in yelling at the grizzled old geezer, who somehow had mysteriously left his seat beside the Emeralds dugout!

After the game, which we lost in extra innings unfortunately, the Eugene Emeralds radio announcers wanted to interview me down on the field. The radio announcers told me that they had seen some long blasts by current major league Home-run Stars Mike Schmidt and Greg Luzinski (Eugene was the Philadelphia Phillies AAA team for years until 1978) but had never seen a ball hit as far or as powerful as that one! Now as fate would have it - I truly believed in Gods sense of humor, because about that time the grizzled old Cincinnati Reds coach, was sauntering by us on the field and didn't act like he noticed me or the radio announcers. Out of character I couldn't help but yell out at him "HEY George - I really had a tough time getting around on your pitcher didn't I"? He stopped for a moment with his back to us and then decided to keep on walking. I explained to the announcers what he had said to me before all of the rage and "ragging" for no reason. After the radio interview I yelled at him once again "HEY George - do you have another Reds hat? The one I my friend stole from you is worn out now"! Life has a way of evening things up - especially in baseball!

Chapter 4

The Injury-Accident

Well darn - the next day - June 20, 1979 - was similar to the day after I hit 4 Home-runs in college. I was still on a wonderful "high" feeling one day and then "down in the dumps" the next. What happened in the 6th inning of the 2nd game of the season at Eugene was something all players hope will not happen to them. A collision at first base involving me, the first baseman, the batter/runner streaking to first base, the umpire attempting to get a good close look at the play and a wild throw. As I got to the bag to receive a possible throw from our 3rd baseman - I noticed that he "short-armed" the throw and the ball was fading into the batter/runner. The batter/runner caught up with the ball just as I stretched my left arm out in an attempt to snag the ball and a split second later we all collided with each other and including the umpire. Hats, helmets, gloves, masks went everywhere as did the 3 of us. I really thought that my left knee was dislodged from my leg, and my left shoulder bent back about 120 degrees so far and hurt the worst, my right elbow and wrist probably from the fall, and my left wrist and hand. I was thinking well; at least I'll have last nights game on Opening Day to remember. I went to the hospital and spent the next day there. The other 2 players in the collision had bad bumps and bruises but would return to action soon. After I got out of the hospital I spent 3 days at my apartment trying to get the swelling down so that I could fly home. The flight home was going to be a challenge as the swelling was down but still there and everything was still as sore as heck. 1 week after Opening Day on June 26th I flew home fighting off pain and the cold sweats in what was an excruciating flight from Seattle to Kansas City.

As the plane landed at KCI I was anticipating my Dad to pick me up at the airport. As I got off the plane and limped into the airport I realized that I needed to go the bathroom really bad. It was a long flight and it was hard as heck for me to unzip my pants in the condition that I was in although I did it getting ready to go to the airport but the pain was nauseating. As I entered the airport I couldn't believe my eyes - but my pretty Peggy was there waiting for me looking as pretty as ever! It was an unbelievable sight for sore eyes as she had on a royal blue shirt and scarf with a light checker blue "over-shirt" and designer like jean shorts. She looked sharp, tan and I could see her beautiful freckles on her face that I love so much! We attempted to hug but it was painful and I had to tell her the really bad news - that I needed someone to help me unzip my pants in the restroom! We both cracked up but I couldn't laugh too hard because I had to go to the bathroom badly and besides it was hard to laugh with all of my injuries. Not to mention the sudden medication that I was on to reduce inflammation.

Well, Peggy just took over the entire airport at that time by charging in and clearing out one of the men's restrooms as we pushed our way in to a stall! She had no problem unzipping me and pulling out my, you know what - so that I could urinate. Normally an embarrassing moment it would have been for both of us - we just did it with her "can do and take charge" attitude. Of course, she had to mention, that she hoped that dinky thing would get a little bit larger at some intimate point in time! We laughed at her joke and just as she was zipping me up wouldn't you know it, someone saunters into the stall right by us, and proceeded to unload in the toilet next to us unmercifully. Needless to say Peggy and I got out of there as quickly as we could and then just about died laughing as we got back into the airport hallway. For a few seconds I forgot about all of my injuries and my pain.

Because Peggy drove her car, I had to lie down in the back seat with my left foot sticking out of the window and my right arm and hand sticking out of the other back window. It was an unbelievable predicament but we actually had a great time talking and catching up and laughing about our airport experience! Peggy said that she turns down the ringer on her phone so that she can sleep and study and forgets to turn up the volume - when I asked her why she doesn't answer her phone. Of course I wanted to know if the number was still good. And when my mom calls for Peggy - she gets her right away - thinking that it might be nice if Peggy could pick me up at the airport.

And I was so glad that she did and when I got home Peggy stayed with me for several hours as we watched TV and visited. She watched over me like a beautiful bride to be! She mentioned that the next 2 years were going to be extremely busy as she is taking some graduate hours and attempting to solidify herself in her first job.

Peggy also mentioned some family challenges that she is dealing with as well as having occasional migraine and sensory headaches. We talked about marriage - especially when we both get stabilized a bit - hopefully in about 2 years. Peggy said that she wants to be able to give 100% to our marriage so she was hopeful of clearing away the major part of her schooling and settling into her job and hopefully stabilizing an accounting/business career and clearing out some family trauma and drama. I said - what family doesn't have that? And we talked about planning better so that we could get together more often.

Of course for me it looked as if my baseball career is going to be over so now I needed to focus on getting my career going. I had a lead on a YMCA job that would open up in Topeka in the fall. The Topeka YMCA Executive Director Jerry Robertson and I have visited about a possible Y- Career! Jerry was the Washburn Baseball volunteer pitching coach the past 2 years in addition to his duties as the YMCA Executive Director. Jerry and I got to know each other and I really enjoyed his attitude, demeanor and leadership! He was a value oriented person with great people skills. I had a good feeling about this possible opportunity!

Unbelievably and against my parents and Peggy's advice, I actually healed a lot quicker than I thought and went back to Salem to play in about a dozen more minor league games. Because of my previous injuries I did not do well but the team had a rash of injuries after I left and needed someone with experience to "hold down the fort". I was only able to go 6 for 30 and My previous injuries were becoming more and more aggravated with each game so I came home for the last time on August 2nd. This was a sad day for me as my dreams of playing professional baseball were now over. It was a sad day for the baseball world as New York Yankee Catcher Thurman Munson died piloting his plane near Columbus, Ohio.

Life at 24, after 2 of your dreams are over?

Sadly - I did not yet know it - but I would never see my Peggy ever physically in human form, on this earthly plane again. It is unbelievable to think that this would be true in the fall of 1979. I was very satisfied with Peggy and our recent conversation (s) that we were both going to be busy attempting to identify our career paths - and that we would see the light at the end of the tunnel in about 2 years and live happily ever after!

In August of 1979 I landed a job with Kansas Neurological Institute coaching young adult boys and girls with slight mental retardation. It was an extremely fulfilling and rewarding job as you can imagine. The goal for these young adults was to get them ready to live in their own apartments so they could live an independent life. The clients all called me "coach"! I was also helping "coach" my friend Dick Dodson as we traveled to small towns in Kansas and Missouri, with the hope of getting Dick hired as a newspaper reporter. It was a fun exercise for me and motivated me to really get focused on my own job and career search! It was a difficult mental adjustment realizing that my professional baseball aspirations were now over. Dick had gone through this adjustment a couple of years earlier and he really helped me with my adjustment.

Of course baseball would still be there for me as I would "drop back down" and play in our local semi-pro baseball league again (what turned out to be 4 more years). But baseball would never have the priority or the focus again as I must give that to my new career - whatever that would turn out to be. And it would end up being a 35 years YMCA administrative career! Jerry Robertson was true to his word and hired me in October of 1979, to be the new Youth Community Director at the YMCA. It was a perfect job (and career) to be able to stumble into. The Youth Community Director was in charge of all YMCA Youth Sports Programs. 1,800 kids in the baseball program, 1,400 in the youth basketball program, 600 in Y Flag Football and we would add other age groups to all of these programs in my 4 years! Securing fields and buildings to play in, recruiting and training coaches, officials and scorekeepers and site supervisors. Additionally I was in charge of 170 acre YMCA Camp Hammond including the parent-child Y-Indian Guides Program. All Y programs included the Y-USA values education emphasizing sportsmanship, fair play, respect for your opponent etc. The score was not emphasized but the development of the youth participants was.

During the summer, if I had my work completed and covered, I was able to play baseball in our old Stan Musial League, with the Topeka 7up Reds and the Topeka Lobos. The Lobos were managed by one of the most interesting persons that I ever met in my life, Jim Shores who was 1/4 African-American- 1/4 Hispanic - 1/4 Caucasian and 1/4 Native American.

Jim Shores was on Lee Dodson's staff at Washburn University and taught criminal justice classes at Washburn University. His classes were amazing and eye opening, especially for a white middle class young college student! Jim grew up hard and was gambling on street corners at a very young age. Much of his youth was spent at Boys-Town in Omaha under the famous Father Flanagan. On Sunday afternoons Jim would invite me to play with the Lobos against Leavenworth or Lansing Prison teams, if I did not have a game with the Topeka Aces or the Topeka 7up Reds. It was quite an education in reality to say the least. Later in life I think a lot about Jim Shores and the difficult life that he had and yet he was always giving back! I read his book on Malcom X and toured Malcom X home in Omaha - and again was humbled about my middle class life in Topeka, Kansas. I was lucky to have amazing mentors in my life like Lee Dodson, Jerry Robertson, Alex Grieves, George Tompkins, Leonard Worthington, Louie Warren, Rich Schoffelman and I was honored to have strong friends of color who helped and assisted me in my life journey like Jim Shores, Ron Epps, Joe M Hill among others. My life has always been truly blessed!

My goal of getting established with My YMCA job that was turning into a career that was going very well and I was really working hard at it - while at the same time having a lot of fun! Still young enough to play a lot of pick up basketball, tennis and 2 new sports at the Y - Handball and racquetball! I was also jogging and still playing semi-pro baseball at a high competitive level - and working a lot of fun 12-14 hour days at the Topeka YMCA! I was having a blast, staying busy, learning a lot and getting educated with both my Y-work and through the YMCA Career Development Program (CDP). The YMCA Career Development Program helped push the Y-Movement to the head of the class when it came in relation to other not for profit and even for profit organizations. The Y-USA Training and Education system was second to none! For once I really studied during these 3-10 day (12-14 hour day) sessions that educated and taught us how to manage and operate a YMCA from Board, volunteer and staff recruitment and training, fiscal management, fundraising - both capital and sustaining, membership recruitment and development, program development, building maintenance, building design and remodeling, organizational structure development and management, special event focus, etc.

Happily busy in my late twenties - the one sad thing missing from my life was my Peggy. If I had a few seconds to think I could not figure out how in the heck did I lose her again, why did this keep happening, and how can I get her back into my life? I often felt twinges, intuitions, ESP, telepathic communication from Peggy so why can't we be together? Obviously my early years in the YMCA were important for helping me develop an administrative career path that led me to becoming a YMCA Association "turn around manager"! It was a label that I really liked and eventually promoted myself with this label. Still being young and idealistic with the 4 core YMCA Values - Caring, Honesty, Respect and Responsibility - as well as the early history of Christian values in Y programs made me feel passionate about this wonderful worldwide organization! Using my baseball training energy worked extremely well regarding my early YMCA focus. This really helped me learn a lot about the many areas of the YMCA that a Y skilled staff person needed to know. Of course the biggest area of learning is the old fashioned "School of hard knocks". I was certainly getting my dose of learning! My career path led me to Little Rock after 4 years as the Youth Community Director with the Topeka YMCA. My first career move was to turn around 2 branches with the YMCA of Little Rock. It took

4 years and then I went to Plainview, Texas and was the Executive Director of that Independent Y Association for 4 years!

With a sister reeling from a husband that left her with 3 teenagers, Lissa moved back to our hometown of Topeka so I took advantage of a Y Downtown Branch opening in Wichita so that I could be close enough to assist her. Even though it was a bit of a drop in status regarding my career path, we turned around the Downtown Y in Wichita, Kansas into a spectacular facility in the next 4 years. In 1994 I went back to west Texas for 3 years to turn the Odessa Family Y around. Then I went up to Omaha to experience a bit of a different environment with a fast growing association for 3 years!

During all of these years - My thoughts about Peggy often would come up and often at the oddest times such as in 1985 when I was pitching for the Little Rock Chiefs. In my windup and on top of the mound and about to deliver the big pitch (in a big game) of the game - my Peggy appeared to me in a very sexy bikini by a waterfront! (Playing in 1985 and 1986 for the Little Rock Chiefs semi-pro baseball team in the all black (except me) Arkansas semi- pro League! I was able to play on Saturday and Sunday afternoons! I broke the color barrier for the league and I had a blast) At that time at age 31 and 32, when I thought that my baseball days were over, Peggy appeared at various times to me during ballgames, racquetball, tennis and handball games just when the games would hit their hot focal points! These moments are similar to times for example while jogging I would be in the state they call "runner highs". Remember, Peggy is alive in human form during these times! I always, for example, have felt Peggy standing beside and/or behind me during important board meetings, or at church, and at Optimist Club meetings, etc. There is no doubt in my mind that Peggy knew where I was but I could not figure out where she was physically on this earth plane. Therefore, analyzing the difficult time that I had finding her years later make it seem as though we were not supposed to be together in this lifetime. The hard thing for us to accept as we live out our lifetimes in this physical 3D world is that we have had lifetimes before and will have after either on earth or other similar planets and venues. Peggy and I have been together before and I believe that we agreed to be apart, this one time, because we had things to learn - and these things needed to be learned without the help or interference of our romantic soul mate.

As the years moved on for me in 1983, I was becoming interested in spreading my YMCA professional wings and was looking at job possibilities within the YMCA national system. My wonderful first 3+ years was so amazing and so awesome as Jerry Robertson had built a wonderful staff team that was so similar to the Topeka Aces baseball teams that I played on! As a Y-professional staff team we worked together as a team, we respected each other and each other's talents and we pitched in for each other in times of challenge and in times of need. The way that our staff team worked at the Topeka YMCA is the way that all YMCA, non-profit and for profit staff teams should work. Jerry Robertson was the best YMCA Executive Director/CEO that I ever saw in my 35 years of YMCA work. I always would attempt to reach the pinnacle of our Topeka YMCA staff teams with the YMCA's that I managed and organized in my Y-career. I came close a couple of times but never did we have the staff team equal to our Topeka staff team from 1979-1983.

Jerry Robertson was heading to Washburn University in 1983 to become the Athletic Director and his replacement at the Topeka YMCA was shall I say, less than ideal. Therefore, the reality of the real world was beginning to come into focus that our "Camelot" period of almost 4 years at the Topeka YMCA was not as "normal" as I thought it was. This wonderful period of my life was coming to an end and I would never experience a "Camelot" period again. The unique situation that we were in from 1979-1983 is now viewed by all of us, as a time we can "treasure" and one that we can strive for, even if the odds are long about ever achieving it again. Because of this, several staff began to look at other opportunities, both inside and outside of the YMCA. My opportunity was going to come at the YMCA of Little Rock where I was hired to be the Southwest YMCA Branch Executive Director! I was really excited about this opportunity that began in October of 1983.

My schedule of working 10-12 hour days continued with my new position in LittleRock! I was really motivated and fired up to prove that I could manage a YMCA Branch and had the youth, training, enthusiasm and energy to prove myself! Therefore, I almost but not quite, forgot about my Peggy. However, she was not completely out of my mind, and I was still receiving subtle intuitive feelings from her! During my first week vacation in May of 1984, I tried 1 more time to find my dream-girl. I spent Memorial week in Topeka with my parents and friends but also spent time looking for Peggy, who I had a tip, was living in the Lawrence area. I spent a full day in Lawrence again visiting with friends and attempting to get more clues about Peggy. On the second day I drove to Lawrence on Highway #24, as I liked to take the scenic route, it was a bright and sunny day and I was still hopeful of finding my Peggy. About halfway to Lawrence out of no-where was a scary and weird-crash sounding loud noise that was like a combination of a thunder-clap and dropped dishes in the high school cafeteria. It was a finger-nail on the chalk-board kind of noise. And it came out of nowhere with hardly any cars on the road or anyone around anywhere. Along with the loud clap I received a telepathic type message telling me not to pursue Peggy. It was the kind of message that actually scared me to death and really saddened me. I did turn around my car and drove back to Topeka immediately not to really give up on pursuing Peggy, but to attempt to process in my mind about what had just happened.

After a few days, except for an occasional image and memory of Peggy off and on over the next 30+ years until August of 2018. This occurrence/encounter was not the first one for me regarding a young lady that I was interested in. Close to 10 years earlier, a young lady I was flirting with and very interested in, asked me out for a date. At that time the custom was for the guy to ask the girl out but this young lady became tired of waiting for me to ask her out and decided to ask me out. It was at Washburn University's Learning Resource Center building in 1984 after a history class. It was actually a dream come true for me at that time but much to my surprise, I responded with something like "Oh, I am sorry, but I cannot go out right now, but Thanks for asking"! Needless to say the young lady was surprised and disappointed. What I said to this young lady was not true as I really wanted to go out with her and had wanted to for several months. Somehow and someway someone else took over my brain/mouth and gave this young lady "my" answer. I was both amazed, saddened and yet very intrigued at what just happened to me. I actually sensed that my guardian angels led by God, we're watching over me and took the decision making process out of my hands.

Today I would say that it must have been my divine spirit team, my angels and spiritual guides approved by our creator. Because I felt a strange peace and had a peaceful feeling after this occurrence, I was actually OK with what happened and I thanked God for the guidance he was giving me in my life. Sometimes we do not get the answer that we want to hear but if we keep the faith in guidance from the divine, other better opportunities will come our way! This kind of situation happened a few times with my YMCA career path in that I would see a YMCA job opening that I think that I wanted and the divine timing was not ready just yet.

But when I had time to think about my life and about Peggy, which was not very often, I was still very frustrated about my inability to find Peggy, and having this very strange loud scary noise experience happen to me as I was driving on Highway #24 to Lawrence, I took it as my God and guardian angels guiding me once again. This occurrence with Peggy was much harder to accept however, then my previous experience with the young lady in the Learning Resource Building, because Peggy seemed like the perfect fit for me - mentally, physically, emotionally and most of all - Spiritually.

Because of my busy schedule and being motivated to start my YMCA Professional Career on a good note, Including establishing myself with a good beginning history of professional work, I begrudgingly put Peggy aside, at least until I had some time to absorb, contemplate and process all of any information regarding Peggy. I just did not want to ever give up on her and I do not think that she wanted to give up on me either. But why would this happen (again) and why could I not find her and will I ever see her again? Living in the prime of my life on the earthly plane made things hard to have the spiritual perspective that I needed. At 67 years old now with some education of spirituality and the world around it gives me a much more complete and understanding perspective of my life and for everything "Peggy".

Often, when I decided; against my own will, to attempt to put "Peggy" aside, I would suddenly receive the occasional, happy, positive, calming, warm Love intuitions and telepathic Love thoughts that seemed to be coming from her. Thus, I would ask myself, "Why did they seem to come from her and why can't I find her"? Again I tried to tell myself that God is guiding me and to Trust in the Lord our God! And again I suppose that the good news is that I did not have the time to contemplate all of this a lot, because of my busy YMCA work schedule. However, my conversations with my mom, and sometimes my dad (my mom and dad just loved Peggy also - she just like a daughter to them) would almost always circle back to knowledge of Christian Science, the Spiritual side of our being, even of ESP, tarot and oracle, fortune telling, etc. Much of this kind of thinking was viewed by society as "quackery" and with not much relevance to the "real world". I never understood how "we" earthlings accept the Middle East and Christian wars, white man's ruthless rule of the native Americans and the African Americans, the KKK etc, but oh don't go to the occult or the topics of spiritual intuition, angels and spiritual guides. Peggy, to her credit always seemed as though she had some kind of "higher self-realization", and gave me the feeling that there was a lot more there than meets the eye (of course knowing her in my early twenties - all that was there for the eyes to see was pretty good too). She was so polite, so respectful and so quiet and humble that it was not hard to believe that she was also a very good student and talented cheerleader.

Time was beginning to move on for me and in 1987 I made another career move to become the Executive Director of the Plainview YMCA. My career path was really beginning to grow in a very positive direction and my reputation was building. After 4 really fun and wonderful years in west Texas, where the people are so incredibly nice, I moved to Wichita, Kansas to manage the Downtown

YMCA. This downtown Y needed an image change and was right in the middle of the pro-life and pro- choice forces, and the "Crips and Bloods" gangs were nearby and really creating bedlam. It was 1991 and downtown Wichita was almost a "sur-real" experience. Because of my busy Y-Career and baseball, my romantic life suffered greatly. Of course part of that was because I was still hopeful in finding Peggy, even though I was thinking of her less and less and she was "coming through" less and less. My dates would almost never get anywhere because deep down I did not want to give up on Peggy. In Little Rock and in Wichita I had a few close call romances that never had the passion that I would have had with Peggy. Thus, potential long term relationships were dismissed early with my career path moving quickly, and my occasional thoughts of my Peggy. Boy I missed her and would have really enjoyed her calm support in my early years with the YMCA.

Chapter 5

Danette and Peggy – What a lucky guy!

So when I met Danette ("my earth wife") Tipton in 1993. Danette was working for United Way and I had been the Executive Director of the Downtown YMCA for almost 2 years now. We had both been through past and recent broken relationships and we were ready for "rebounded romance". Danette is from Wichita and our parents both attended Emporia State University. Danette is a non-profit - cause driven star having been one of the first to work with and stay with aids patients in the 1980's. College friends remember her unabashed crusade to get friends to wear condoms. She had also been a program director for Big Brothers and Big Sisters. Our non-profit careers seemed to be a good connection for us. Looking into our future, we both would need each other for our Executive Director and CEO pursuits. Non profit agencies in those days had Boards of Directors that were 99% white and 90% male. They wanted to hire "Normal" white heterosexual CEO's who had reputations of staying out of trouble. Because of this and our solid if not commendable work history, our professional careers grew because of our marriage! If the romance and the passion of couples getting hitched at younger more common ages, the stability of our marriage relationship has been a real advantage for both of us!

As Danette's "earth husband"" - One of the things that Danette and I have shared in common is the admiration for James Van Praagh, who we watched on the "Larry King Live" show in the 1990's. James is a highly intelligent and intuitive Psychic Medium who brought communicating with souls who passed over to the TV! Danette and I caught several JVP appearances on Larry King and began to notice that several other Psychics were selling books, making appearances on TV and radio and were beginning to explode on the internet. Best selling authors Deborah King, Sonia Choquette, Dougall Frazier, Radleigh Valentine and other have just exploded with the basic theme that "we are spiritual beings living a human existence" and not the other way around. This is something that my mother, June O Lord predicted would happen way back in the 1970's. My mother studied Christian Science and Metaphysical Christianity with Emmet Fox and even Norman Vincent Peale as well as the great ministry at Unity Village, Missouri. As my (and Danette's) education of these wonderful spiritual leaders increased so to has the verification of earlier personal thinking and common sense problem solving. Despite challenges of busy work schedules and high level responsibilities of managing and administrating large non-profit organizations, Danette and I have managed our marriage in much the same way as we have managed our agencies. Using our dogs as our spiritual connectors we have been able to get through the normal challenges that couple go through in today's world. If the romance of younger couple is missing the Love, friendship, respect and support has been there.

Danette is one of the most passionate advocates of civil rights, women's rights, children's rights, animal rights and people's rights! She has led me to focus and to become more passionate myself on some of these issues even if I agreed with her advocacy in all of these areas and more. Danette was the first Executive Director of a Child Advocacy Center to be able to leave the local job in one city and move into the same job in another city. It is something done in YMCA movement but not many other non-profit organizations use the experience and training advantage to hire someone with a good Executive record from the same national organization. Child Advocacy Centers deal with child sexual abuse and it is truly a crisis organization. Almost all of the non-profit organizations that Danette has managed including Big Brother Big Sister, Rape Crisis Center and March of Dimes are crisis organizations. My YMCA career was mostly a preventative organization that might happen to deal with occasional crisis situations. The challenge of managing YMCA's is the sheer volume of people that you have to deal with in an effective and efficient way. But outright crisis management that Danette's agencies deal with on a daily basis, is normally not part of the YMCA menu thank goodness.

Spiritually Danette is a believer in the spiritual realm but hesitates to incorporate that knowledge at the rapid pace that I have in the last 5 years. Danette is coming around to the fact that we, as Sonia Choquette unabashedly and without hesitation professes that "we have angels and spirit guides around us all of the time - so talk to them and get to know them!" We all have 1 or 2 guardian angels, normal angels, spirit guides including finding those with the specialties that we currently need and we can ask them for help - even with certain problems. We as human beings are not utilizing anywhere near the available resources that we have available to us in any way, shape or form! We also don't use resources such as wonderful spiritual businesses such as "California Psychics" who can put us in touch with psychic mediums of all backgrounds and abilities to help us with our day to day challenges, career guidance and advice, romance, future projections, getting rid of negative energies and negative influences on the spiritual side, help with past life recognition and extermination of bad karma and energies from past lives!

So it is an amazing, but not surprising, revelation that all of my (and Danette's) recognition of all of this spiritual age is coming at a time in the collective universe that is celebrating the beginning of the "Age of Aquarius" - happening right now in 2020 and 2021! So it is not surprising that both Danette and I have found out that we both have romantic Spiritual Guides waiting for us on the "Spiritual side"! Danette and my marriage and friendship and spiritual discovery, has happened so that we could support each other with like minded beliefs and help each other with our professional careers, cementing our friendship and karma into the ages! What a wonderful revelation this has been for both of us - as our soulmates, both on the "other side" now, wait for us so that we can someday incarnate back to earth to learn more lessons (or to possibly incarnate to some other place in the universe)! Actually, our romantic soulmates are very busy on the other side with activities and job like responsibilities! Listening to recent James Van Praagh Facebook and you tube and internet program broadcasts, it is obvious that the "in-between world" is similar to what we experience here on earth. People have fun activities, goals and objectives they set in consultation with their spirit guides, workshops, seminars, baseball games, recreational activities - all with the goal of improving our individual selves and to contribute positively to the collective and universal world that we live in.

The difference between those of us living here on earth and those on the spiritual side is like the difference of radio frequencies. That is why some people, for example the psychic-mediums with California Psychics, are more in tune and able to communicate easier and freer with those on "the other side". Psychic mediums have more developed chakra systems - especially the thymus and 3rd eye areas. The #1 message people tell us from the other side is that we do not die. Our spirit lives on and it is only our earthly bodies that wear out. People on the other side encourage us to bless our bodies and thank it for its service to us but to toss it aside as if it were an old overcoat! On the other side we are healed and can look like ourselves at the age we want to look! How Cool is that! When I started connecting with Peggy on the other side our psychic mediums said that Peggy is getting younger by the day and often wears her Cheerleading uniform when she visits me! How fantastic and fun is that! When I listen to the James Van Praagh Friday night series every Friday last fall - people coming through were having a great time! They were healing, attending workshops and lectures, playing cards and enjoying and supporting each other! People were playing the piano and planting flowers and attending concerts, etc. The vibration level is higher than on earth and thus is much more positive than the low vibrations we sometimes let ourselves lapse into here on earth.

Danette has always had a passion for Civil rights, fairness and equality as well as all of the virtues listed above. I am sure that my connection with her is to help me be more empathetic in all situations. I was raised to have compassion and show compassion and I believe that it is natural for me to be compassionate. Danette, however, has taught me the deeper and more thorough meaning of compassion and empathy. No one gets a pass in this life but some definitely have a more difficult time than others. One of Danette's recent hobbies and classes is drawing and art and she has begun to draw famous negro men in our history like Fredrick Douglas and Martin Luther King. It was shortly after she began drawing these famous black historical figures when it was revealed to me that Danettes romantic soul-mate did not incarnate in this life but was a black, well decorated lawyer, in their last lifetime together! Because of race issues at that time, they could not live together in the same house. It is an amazing coincidence that this discovery came at the same time that she had started drawing profiles of the famous black men!

As my 35 year YMCA career finished up on December 1, 2014, Danette was working only on a part time basis also. We decided to explore areas that we might like to live so we spent a year and a half in Surprise, Arizona and a yearned and a half back in Mobile, Alabama. We really enjoyed discovering both areas of the country but decided to come home to Wichita, Kansas in July of 2018 so that we could be close to Danette's parents who are still alive and in their 80's. It was in late July and early August of 2018, when I decided to volunteer at the National Baseball Congress Semi-Pro Baseball Tournament! It is the same Tournament that has been hosted in Wichita's "Lawrence-Dumont" Stadium since 1935! It is the same tournament that I played in with the Topeka Aces 1973-1976 and it is the same tournament that my Peggy saw me and the Topeka Aces play in 1975 and 1976.

Thus in the last and final year of this amazing baseball tradition and the wonderful Lawrence-Dumont Stadium, that memories suddenly began flowing into my mind and my spirit from more than 40 years ago. Helping out at this nostalgic old baseball venue that thoughts, memories and intuitions of Peggy came flooding back into my mind again! As I mentioned, in the last 40 years, an occasional thought or intuition, would come into my mind at the oddest times - when, unfortunately, I would simply dismiss it. The flood of memories of my teammates, coaches, games and Peggy came to me more and more, each day of this 10 day baseball tournament. It was wonderful and sad and nostalgic all at the same time. My personal range of emotions was up and down and all around as with each day more and more of my thoughts and thinking was about my Peggy.

With this experience of volunteering at the 2018 NBC Baseball tournament I had a new and heightened awareness of Peggy, but continued to dismiss these thoughts as "just one of those things that happens in a lifetime". For the next year and 3/4 Peggy kept coming back into my mind with more regularity. I found myself putting off these thoughts and yet coming back to them over and over again. And then I would attempt to analyze each of us and analyze how we missed the opportunity of spending our life together. As these thought became more and more persistent I began to try to look up Peggy on line, in an effort to find out what happened to her. I could not find her and I kept thinking how incredibly elusive Peggy was in all of our lives. At this point of time in 2019 and early 2020 Peggy was a bitter-sweet memory but my curiosity kept increasing about what in the world has happened to her? Then came the a typical spring Kansas thunder and lightening storm on the night of April 28 th, 2020! Everything changed more dramatically than in my wildest dreams - and I knew that My Peggy was Back into my life Again!

It was a huge Thunder-Clap that almost knocked me out of my living room rocker at 7:45pm! Along with the Thunder and Lightening clap I had a vision of Peggy turning over our outdoor table as the glass top shattered into a million pieces! Full Speed ahead like a speeding Locomotive Peggy came into my mind with incredible power! It was full of high definition messages, pictures and images! I was in awe of the power and yet the calm feeling but determined intuition that I had! I knew that I was in for the most wonderful ride of my life!

Chapter 6

Music with Peggy and my friend Danny Gans

There are several other instances now that I can remember mainly between 2017 and April 28, 2020 but I never even thought of Peggy as I had no idea where she was or had been. But I do know that it was a very soft and loving feeling that would come through my intuition just like the Field of Dreams! During this time frame I began purchasing Spiritual books from Unity, Louise Hays, James Van Praagh, Dougal Frazier, Rayleigh Valentine, Deborah King and others at an accelerated pace. My foundation was built with the Episcopal Prayer Book, Mary Baker Eddy and Christian Science, Dr. Emmet Fox and Norman Vincent Peale - all who touched on life after death and our Spiritual self being our true self. Then Raymond Moody wrote "Life after Life" which was the first major best-selling book that directly approached the subject during the 1980's. I know that Peggy accelerated my somewhat latent belief that our souls never die and that there is "Life after Life".

I truly believe that Peggy's soft guidance also led me to re-discover the music of our years in College and on the baseball diamonds in the 1970's. In order of discovery I am listing them along with fairly current new-age music here: 1) the new age album "Believe" by Thomas Lemmer with song titles of "Soul-Diver" "Is it too late" "coming home" "Above the clouds" "Floating" "Never let me Go" "There is Hope" "Behind the strange signal". Peggy was definitely speaking to me with this Awesome new age album released in the 1990's.

Then there were some of our old favorites: one of the many of Steve Miller Band - our favorite "Keep on Rockin me - and instead of baby - I would insert "Peggy" while I drove and sang to her as she covered her ears with both hands not wanting to take in the beauty of my singing voice. The wonderful Boston album release in 1977, was a huge favorite of our as was the Alan Parson Project.

Native Chill is a fairly recent new-age album that I began playing while driving in 2018 and 2019 by David Arkenstone. When the song "Spirits are Calling" I remember, and still do, get "goosebumps" and I wasn't sure why? Also song titles that have much more meaning to me now - "Children of the moon" "Ghost-runner"

"Dream of the Shaman"! There is no doubt in my mind that Peggy guided me to this album and those songs.

During the dating days of our college years Peggy was much more hip than my music fav's such as "Peter Gunn" and "Mr Lucky" and she liked most of my new age and current pop songs entire album of the "Heart and "Fleetwood Mac" and the song "Dreamweaver" really gave me chills and does to this day. I was always a new-age guy with "Spra-gyra" and Jon Luc Ponte and as mentioned in the 1st book - I am a terrible dancer. Peggy's remark always was "I can see why your mom, who taught piano lessons with a student load of well over 100, let me get off after only 2 weeks of lessons".

Peggy really liked to dance and I Loved watching her dance so out of desperation she developed this dance routine that we tried out at some way out of the way dance club that might be termed a "Biker-Bar" in the country. In fact she had to drive to get to it because I had no idea where it was - somewhere between Topeka and her home area of Iola, Kansas. Peggy felt comfortable here which made me wonder what kind of folks she grew up with. But everyone was really nice and once they got to know me they would ask me baseball questions. Peggy would dress me up with an old tie and suit coat and some kind of goofy hat and my job was basically to stand there and look amused while she did this wild cheerleader type dance routine rotating around me. I guess that I got so good at being the "straight-guy" that I began receiving compliments about what a good dancer I was becoming!

Other albums and songs that hit me hard when I hear them now because of the strong memories of Peggy and I in the 1970's are: The 5th Dimension with the "Dawning of the Age of Aquarius" which has even more significant meaning now than it did in 1969, as does one of their songs "Don't you Hear me Calling to ya" and of course I Love their version of "Sunshine of your Love" that Jimi Hendrix made famous. And we both like my brother John's favorite - Brazil 66 with "Going out of my Head over you" and "Like a Lover" and of course the "Look of Love". Peggy went wild along with my parents when Peggy Lee's hit song came out "Is that all there is" - then let's keep dancing, bring out the booze and have a ball! My parents nor Peggy and especially me were not drinkers but that song resonated with my parents especially and they and Peggy would dance around the house making all kinds of weird noises and sounds while I watched in disbelief with my mouth wide open!

When I hear the "Simple Minds" album I get goose-bumps and Peggy will come through my intuition extra strong especially with "All the things she said - she said" and "Don't you forget about me" as well as "See the Lights"!

Because Peggy came to me "out of the blue" as far as my conscious state of being was at the time, April 28, 2020, when the Police song title of "Message in the bottle" hits home so much that I now always have tears in my eyes. And Patrick O'Hearn's album "Between 2 Worlds" makes me wonder if he is like me - realizing that we are now communicating in 2 or more worlds?

But the "coup de gras" is when I hear the Cranberries song "Zombie". Forget Northern Ireland, that song was made in an attempt to make the entire world think about our "Guns and our Bombs and our Bombs and our Guns". One of my past life discoveries was that, believe it or not, I was Oswald and Peggy was Agatha and our 4 year old daughter Olga (a name that we thought was cute from our 2 names) and we all died Jewish at one of the Auschwitz camps. I went first in an effort to extend Agatha's and Olga's lives. Olga had "special powers" according to the Nazi's as she was Psychic. Olga, now Psychic Namath with the awesome business of California Psychics, channels for Peggy and me. Psychic Namath is so gifted at channeling that when I "talk" to Peggy - it is like sitting at the local coffee shop and visiting!

I found out that I was shot to death in an attempt to find Agatha and Olga at one of the Auschwitz camps. I knew that they were near me but did not escape by the Nazi's in 1942 while Agatha and Olga were gassed in or in 1944 or 1945. Patton came through in 1945. Psychic Namath, ie Olga, tells me that Peggy, ie Agatha, was such a good mom - that she, Olga, never felt afraid! One time when the Nazi's came to get me and take me to the rock piles, Olga yelled to me "It's OK - Pa-Pa. Things will turn out OK"!

So when I hear the song "Face down in the moment" by Nathanial Rateliff - it has a completely different meaning to me than it did to him when he wrote the song. Because my Spiritual Guides do not let me "feel" the agony and torture again. I saw it as if I was a bystander. It is so humbling to know that we were in Auschwitz and died there with so many good and wonderful people. Danette had an awesome experience while we were living in the Phoenix area a few years ago. She was driving around a few survivors of Auschwitz and the holocaust. Their stories, as children, were horrific.

Now on to the Lighter-Side - happier side combining baseball and comedy and show business. A wonderful friend I met in my very first minor league baseball experience in the spring of 1978 was Danny Gans "The man of many voices"! Danny was my roommate for the first week of tryouts for the Class A, Victoria Mussels, of the Class A Northwest Minor League. The Northwest League was full of Hollywood ownership money and interests in 1978 and 1979 as Independent Minor League Baseball, making a comeback after a long history of being an important part of Minor League baseball. The Northwest League had 4 Independent teams in the 8 team Northwest League that season. Injured players like myself, and players with good records in other sports and multi-talented celebrities, like Danny Gan's, who might also be good baseball players, we're being given a baseball chance again!

For Danny Gans, a talented musician, comedian and actor, the chance of living his real dream was to good to pass up! Gan's connections with Hollywood as well as his fine College Baseball credentials, helped him receive a tryout with the Victoria Mussels. Ed Charles, former Major League 3rd baseman and New York Mets scout, helped me get a tryout with the Victoria Mussels.

In the first book, I explained that I performed at a level I had never been able to realize, in the 10 day tryout camp. Danny Gans was a switch-hitting 3rd baseman with power, but seems to have a hard time making contact. At 3rd base, Danny seemed stiff and out of practice, but the potential was there for a well rounded player!

As a performer Danny had an incredible singing voice and always entertained us on the long minor league bus rides! Danny would grab the bus drivers microphone and entertain everyone with "the Danny Gans Show" after the last game of a 4-5- or 6 game series against a Northwest League opponent! More of a comedy show then displaying his amazing singing voice, Danny would often review the highlights of the week with a sports show type commentary, often aided by 2-3 enterprising players with sports announcing aspirations! Then Danny would "Roast" a player or 2, sometimes and would even interview himself for a muffed play or lousy decision on the base paths, or even mischief/misconduct in the locker room or practice fields. This was all welcome entertainment late at night as the Victoria Mussels bus would head to Eugene or Salem, Bend or Portland, Oregon and Bellingham or Grays Harbor, Washington.

Travel was particularly challenging for our Victoria Mussels baseball team as we had to get on the ferry-boat express on Vancouver Island. We of course, being temporary Canadian citizens, had to go through customs before landing in Seattle Harbor to begin the land portion of the road trip! All of this gave time for Danny Gans to "hone his craft" as an entertainer that would result in a distinguished career including multiple "Las Vegas Entertainer of the Year Awards"! He was a Las Vegas staple for years along with Wayne Newton!

I fortunately, was able to escape the embarrassment of being roasted for most of the season, until I was just about the last one standing who had not been scalded with the Humorous-Rath of the unofficial "Danny Gans' show. That is until the night of the game in Grays Harbor, when Bill Murray and the Saturday Night Light crew, filmed a show at our Minor League Baseball game, against Grays Harbor. This is the game I wrote about in book #1, when Peggy and her friends drove all of the way from Kansas to see me play as they intermingled with the Saturday Night Live production crew as well as Pete Ward and other Major League scouts!

You may recall that Peggy and I were able to visit and talk and even smooch a bit before our team bus was to leave for a long nighttime road trip to Bend, Oregon. In other words it was going to be a long trip as it would be for Peggy and her friends who turned around to drive back to Kansas. As I was the last one to get on the bus because I did not want to leave "my Peggy". When I finally had to get on the bus I did receive several "Hi-5's" from everyone as I was trying to reclaim my accustomed seat near the back of the bus. I tried to get back there as quietly and softly as I could - but not tonight for Danny Gans had already taken over the microphone and was frothing at the mouth waiting to christen me into the aforementioned "Danny Gans Show"! I thought that I might have escaped but kissing my beautiful Peggy before boarding the bus had not gone unnoticed by Danny Gans or my other teammates.

As I tried to slip down the aisle, loud and clear Danny Gans came through the bus PA system as if I was trying to sneak by the principles office at McCarter Elementary School. Loud and clear I heard "Chasley Lord - where do you think you are going"? As my teammates roared, as they knew what was coming and it was going to be good - they knew that! And because I was on top of the world finding out that my Peggy had come all of this way to see me play, and still having a good, if not frustrating game hitting 4 rockets - good for only 1 Double, I was feeling unusually confident about my upcoming responses to Danny Gans on the Danny Gans show!

My teammates continued to imbibe by drinking the cheapest least expensive beer found anywhere, and on empty stomachs because there weren't any restaurants left open after 10:00. Thus, soaking up the cheap and inexpensive beer were Kwik-Shop vending machine sandwiches the only dinner choice, other than 100 day old Bar-B-Que potato chips. My teammates were roaring - wanting to know more about the beautiful Cheer-leader that had come to see me play!

Gans began editorializing by saying "it is always the quiet ones isn't it guys"? "My teammates went wild with that comment of course! "Chasley Lord" (was the nickname they gave me) quietly comes to the ballpark, get his work done on the field, they are nice to everyone, nobody questions their morals, ethics, sex-life or anything". They crescendo builds from my ballplayers teammates! So, who is this Beauty? Trying to play the country bumpkin I respond - why - that is my Peggy - from Washburn University - she's a "Washburn Ichabod"! Gans: "We can tell she has a great bod- what do you think - we are blind"? No - I responded "Washburn University Ichabods - that is our nickname! Gan's "so where is that"? Me: "Why that school is in Toooepeka, Kaaaansas"! My teammates are now roaring and drinking more cheap beer by the second. Gans: Where is Peggy from? Me: She's from Iola! Gans: Iola - Where is that? Me: Near Halstad and Caker City! "You know - the town with the worlds biggest ball of twine"! My teammates were Now totally unplugged from reality! They were Absolutley delirious with cheap beer filled happy bedlam! Living the dream as they drifted further and further into oblivion with their beer drinking taking over their senses. Gans: Let's go back to Washburn University. What is Washburn University's nickname? Me: "The Ichabods"! Gans: "The What"? Then I changed it a bit to "The Great Bods"! You have to have a Great "Bod" to go there! Teammates just about pummel me with that one as I got lifted and tossed like a mash-pit back into the back of the bus so that: I was then told by Danny Gan's to "take my seat and be quiet" the rest of the trip!

Of course, because Danny and I were roommates for the first week of tryout camp, he knew most of what came out in my roasting interview that night. A funny phone call from Peggy happened on about day 3 of our tryout camp, early in the season. Peggy telephoned the team office and received the number of the phone in our room. Danny Gans gift that led him to several Las Vegas Entertainer of the Year Awards, was that he could imitate all time great singers such as Frank Sinatra, Dean Martin, Perry Como, Sammy Davis Junior and others! Danny had an incredible talent to pick up voice patterns easily and quickly. So when Peggy called the connection wasn't the greatest and it was really Danny Gans Peggy was talking to a somewhat crackling sounding Charlie Lord. As Peggy knew, my singing voice was nothing to write home about and as I mentioned, she often covered her ears when I would sing to her! However, this time Danny ie me, begins with small talk with his "very-fresh" lines something of the order "I can smell your beautiful perfume tonite - Baby" and "I bet you are wearing something "slinky" tonight! Something totally out of context for me - and when he launched into the song "Let's get NakedTonight" - Peggy later said that she held the phone out and looked at it in dis-belief! When Danny threw the phone at me and I picked up, I tried to go along with his theme and not only struck out badly but cracked up laughing for minutes! Thankfully Peggy was in good humor laughing also asking who is that nut-case you are rooming with?

As the Victoria team bus traveled to Bend, Oregon the bus driver was beginning to weave around at about 3:00 in the morning as the thin mountain roads looked straight down the side of mountains with little or no barrier. I decided to get up and visit with the bus driver when our batboy, aka "Fetus Munster" who looked like Herman Munster's 10 year old son, began throwing up his first attempt at manhood all over the seat - thankfully, that I had just left. A couple of rowdy players had given our 15 year old batboy a couple of joints and a few bottles of beer and we all paid for it having to inhale that lousy "throw-up" smell for the rest of our trip to Bend. Needless to say it would be even a longer night than it had been up to then and when we arrived at 12:00 noon for the first game of our doubleheader that was starting at 1:00 - we were going to have a challenge winning either of these games. And since our regular 2 Catchers had injuries, one a swollen testicle, the other a swollen tonsil, I was pressed into duty by Catching both games of the doubleheader! Luckily, somehow and someway, visions of my Peggy were stuck in my head and got me through the extremely long day and doubleheader! Thank You Peggy!

As I was looking for the Catchers equipment - shin guards, chest protector, catchers mask, and an optional catchers helmet and of course, catchers cup. One of our coaches informed me that one equipment bag and a bag with some of the teams bats and balls, had come loose on top of the bus last night as we were driving through the mountains heading for Bend, Oregon. While I was talking to the bus driver, in an effort to keep him awake, I heard a commotion of some sort in the back of the bus. We were probably 9 miles straight down the mountain I was looking at early at about 3:00 am. A few of my teammates noticed but quickly went back to sleep the best they could. So, I borrowed a set of catchers equipment, from the opponents, the Bend Phillies and we were about ready to begin the doubleheader - finally!

2 significant future MLB ballplayers played in that game as our starting pitcher Dale "the horse" Mahorcic, would get knocked out of the 1st game in the 1st inning. Mahorcic just didn't have it that day, and was probably suffering from a rough night of Minor League road travel. In the minor leagues you have to get creative often so after working on the side with our pitching coach Dave Rogelstat, Dale "the horse" Mahorcic came back and pitched a complete game win in game #2! Mahorcic broke 7 bats with powerful inside movement on his tailing fastball in a 7-2 win for our Victoria Mussels! On the other side, only a year later for the Bend Phillies, a skinny 18 year old shortstop, with an exaggerated "Carl Yastrzemski type" batting stance/ style, Julio Franco, would play an incredible 20 big league seasons! It was when this young Julio Franco like shortstop, Mobil Cox, came to bat that day, that I had a memory of a vision that took me back our neighborhood sandlot baseball field in Topeka, Kansas!!

When I was 10 years old we played sandlot baseball almost everyday of the year. We played sandlot football, basketball and even hockey, but baseball was by far our favorite. My friend Danny McKinney was like an older brother as well as our neighborhood; the West 19th Street Homerun Champion"! I remember telling Danny about a vision I had while playing one of our sandlot baseball games not long after my 10th birthday in 1964! In the vision I was catching in the Minor Leagues! I was playing catcher, which was not a position that I liked at all as a 10 year old in

1964. In 1978 however, I relented to learning the catcher position and there I was, just like Julio Franco in 1979, the vision that I had 14 years later, behind a skinny kid wearing a Phillies uniform. Suddenly, 14 years later in late June of 1978, that vision that I had forgotten about came back to me abruptly seemingly out of nowhere! Holy Cow "look at these incredible goose-bumps I have, showing the umpire! It was incredible and the umpire asked me if I was OK and he made me get some water to drink. Because I had to still focus on the game, I did not let me dwell on the event until late that evening. The overriding feeling that I had was that I was going to be good enough to play Minor League baseball but that I would not get to play Major League Baseball. A few days later I called my sandlot baseball buddy (who I still know today as we celebrate 61 years of our friendship) and he remembered me telling him about the clear picture vision I had in 1964! These visions were not uncommon when I was growing up in Topeka, Kansas. In fact, when I was a pre-schooler, I had them a lot - including knowing what Christmas presents my father was going to bring home for me on Christmas Eve of 1958! Dad was incredulous to say the least! That Christmas of 1958 is one I will remember forever because it was snowing and everyone, including my grandparents, were excited because the Christmas atmosphere was so electric! And, at 4 years of age, I kind of knew what was going on now, and could enjoy my older siblings enjoy Christmas also! It was on Christmas Eve 1958, when I was having telepathic communication with someone, who was reminding me calmly, to be sure to enjoy this wonderful time at Christmas! It was a very safe, happy and calm communication! I was extremely happy and thankful for this communication. 4 years later, which seemed like a lifetime later, in the basement of our new house at 5517 West 19 th Street, Mary the Mother of Jesus metastasized, in our basement, giving me a blessing of protection! She arrived appearing like a mosaic tornado, stayed long enough for a blessing, and left the same way she arrived! The energy was calm yet incredibly powerful! I went to my room and prayed with celebration after that beautiful appearance! It was incredible! I just assumed that this kind of thing happened all the time!

Even though I used to have visions often when I was a child, I really began seeing them often, in my intuition, after Peggy came to me April 28, 2020. Now I have visions of past lives, and in present time frame and fun future life visions fairly often! These began happening oddly, and I still don't know why and haven't figured this out yet, when Peggy told me how she passed away. From April 28, 2020 for almost 5 months, I was pretty sure that Peggy was on the Spirit side, but I was not absolutely sure 100%. Thus, when I would go to Sedgwick County Park for my Walk/Hike, I was kind of looking to see if someone looked like and might be "my Peggy"!

In September of 2020, I had 2 Major Private Psychic Readings that not only confirmed what I was picking up from Peggy was true through my intuition and through telepathic communication in the previous 4 months! These readings also gave me the confidence to really 100% trust myself when my Spiritual intuition began happening frequently. The first reading was with Katy Tarot, and her Powerful Psychic Readings in early September 2020 on you tube! This reading was the Most Wonderful Present I have ever had in my life! I had had a wonderful life full of high points, gifts and presents of all kinds but this reading just absolutely came from God in Heaven! It was so incredible I cannot properly describe it and how I felt receiving it and I have watched over 100 replays of it and the incredible rush of Spiritual Love and Guidance is Awesome! The 2nd reading with my now good friend Barbara, of Light-worker Tarot and Oracle also on You Tube. This reading did reinforce my Katy Tarot reading of a few days earlier but more than half the reading seemed to not make sense and definitely had a mysterious side to it. Barbara and I could not figure it out? Barbara kept trying to decipher it for a few days and visited with her spirit guides and then it all came to her. Peggy had sent us an SOS message for help thus an entirely different reading than the Katy Tarot reading which a reading of confirmation was and blessing. When Barbara began figuring the meaning of the second reading out it became obvious to Barbara, as they had a few intuitive visits together without me, that Peggy was telling her about her death and in fact told Barbara how she was murdered. Peggy did not want me to know this yet because she was afraid what this information might mean to me mentally, emotionally and spiritually. Of course Peggy knew that we had many past lives together which is something I had not learned about yet even though my sub-conscious mind knew and would "act-out" probably. Barbara did an amazing job realizing the information that Peggy was giving us was serious criminal activity with her "ex" who hired a "murderer" to kill her. Peggy had enough of this "ex" and was going to leave him while discovering his criminal business happenings. Peggy herself was a successful business woman using her Business Administration degree from Washburn University to good use. Peggy discovered that her "ex" was involved in criminal business activities and she began living a life of Domestic Violence with threatening intent from her "ex". Thus, on November 8 - Peggy was murdered by a hired killer. (We discovered this recent information working with Barbara and 2 other Psychic Mediums in September of 2022. We know the names of Peggy's "ex" now as well as of her murderer. As I mentioned previously, The Police know them and are watching them as they are involved in criminal activity in Wichita, Albuquerque and Phoenix. Peggy's "ex" kept her bank accounts open as well as her credit cards updated to give the appearance that she is still alive. Peggy's body was stashed away in an out of the way place by the murderer. Early in October of 2020, Barbara said that Peggy wanted to speak to me through Barbara on October 16, 2020 by telephone. This was when Barbara, and Peggy, informed me that not only had Peggy passed away but that she had been murdered and that her case was an unsolved cold-case mystery. Barbara told me that she will not stop until this case is solved and the murderers are brought to justice. Peggy was so concerned for me and my reaction and my well being after hearing this information (which is so typical - Peggy thinks of everyone else first before herself) that she asked me how detailed did I want to know and I of course, shocked and grief stricken at the moment, just asked for the basic version and that I did not want to make her, "my Peggy", feel bad all of a sudden by re-living this horrible event. Peggy told me that she was not in any pain as her death was very short and quick and she had 2 angels escort her up to heaven, a place that we are all familiar with, as our true home in our true soul existence.

Psychic Caleb and Psychic Dove had been preparing me for this news as you never know how someone will react. The fact that Peggy has recovered and advanced in the Spirit world and is doing so much to help others with her expertise of moving energy and healing, has made it much easier for me to accept this shocking news. Psychic's Namath, Dove and Caleb are always telling me how Peggy has the highest white energy around her and how positive she always is and not to worry about her as she is becoming an amazing Angelic Healing force in the upper realms - even above the 5th dimension to the 15 dimension! The 5th dimension is where our souls go after death in our current life in this 3rd dimension experience here on earth. Many times are material oriented selves drop to the 2nd dimension and become all about matter and material objects and possessions. When you get to the 15 dimension and above you are totally a spiritual being who can, as Jesus did, raise the dead and like Moses did, part the sea. Energy movement is the key as everything is energy! In the spirit world energy and thought move very fast, much faster than here in the 3D, thus they shoot right by us most of the time but occasionally we can catch a piece of their thoughts and energies. BTW - we each have our own energy vibration that identifies us, kind of like our finger-prints. Therefore we know each other on the spirit side by our energies and by our thoughts. We all need to get control of our thoughts because they are there for everyone to see in the spirit world.

Chapter 7

Past Life Discoveries

Past Lives Discovered!!! It was 13 months after Peggy came back to me, which was on April 28, 2020 - when "my Peggy from the past" whispered "Peggy Chamberlain" to me in the middle of a powerful Kansas storm, when I was thinking about exploring my past lives. My "Spiritual" learning curve was speeding up for my "Spiritual Education" degree - as I had many wonderful teachers! You tube tarot educational writers and teachers like "Katy Tarot", Barbara Hurst with "Light-worker Tarot and Oracle", Vince and Alicia with "2 Mystic" Tarot and of course James Van Praagh, Deborah King, Radleigh Valentine, Dougal Frazier are just a few of the many I have learned from! Aleah Ames, Nancy Shobe in addition to Psychic Caleb, Psychic Dove and Psychic Namath are my sounding boards as well as channeling with my beautiful Peggy!

With Peggy's encouragement and Psychic Namath (who I would soon find out was our 4 year old daughter "Olga" when we were at one of the Auschwitz encampments. Our names Peggy ie Agatha in our most recent life and me "Oswald" - thus our daughter "Olga", came from both of our names). suggested that I call a past life Psychic Medium specialist. Before to long I called Psychic Dove and could not have made a better choice. My 3 go to Psychic Mediums, Caleb-Namath-and Dove work at "California Psychics". California Psychics is a very impressive business with 350+ Psychics on staff, ready to help the world! It is an amazing business with an Awesome Spiritual mission!

Right "off the bat" (have you ever noticed how many of English sayings come from baseball? Such as "he's out in Left-Field" or He threw us a "curve-ball" or "he needs to step up to the plate")! Psychic Dove took me on a journey of several of my past lifetimes with Peggy! The common theme of these lifetimes were farming during tough and difficult times of which we had many. In all of these times we were husband and wife except 1 when Peggy was the husband and I was the wife! (Poor Peggy) got the short end of the stick in that lifetime! We always seemed to be challenged by the weather and lack of modern tools for farming. Somehow, someway, we would make it! As I viewed these lifetimes that flew by in my mind so quickly, my viewing position was that of a bystander. Thus, I did not have to re-live the hard times again. The lives that I saw with Psychic Dove I was always with Peggy! I have lived approximately 1,000 lives here on earth and Peggy has been in a third of them.

I went through a detailed lifetime with Aleah Ames, who softly and safely hypnotized me so that I could feel more detail of Peggy and my first life together in France 3,500 years ago! It was a farming life, and we enjoyed each other and our families and friends immensely. My death was as an old man in a fairly normal bed, with family all around me. Peggy had passed away a few years earlier. Almost all family and friends of that lifetime have re-connected with me and with each other in other lifetimes.

In each lifetime we live the goal is to Learn and Grow Spiritually while working on our weaknesses as well as at the same time - attempt to enjoy the current lifetime as much as possible! In my opinion we as human beings are way to caught up in the small insignificant details of life. We also spend to much time criticizing others and competing with others. It is so much better if we genuinely cheer and appreciate every persons unique gifts and contributions to the world. These are the lessons I am deriving as I go through my past life reviews.

The other true reality is the people we hurt and injure during a lifetime sometimes sets our progress back for lifetimes. That is why we need to sincerely ask for forgiveness and be sure to forgive those who injure us. The people we hurt physically, mentally and/or emotionally, we will feel the pain X 10 with our immediate past life review after we pass away and transition back into our full spiritual reality. The myth of competition that has morphed into "cut-throat" competition during my lifetime, makes you better with the "survival of the most fit" is a joke and often leads into an unbalanced person. God provides amply for everyone! There is no limit to our potential success regardless of the so called "competition and/or competitors" because we all can grow as individuals and as a team (whether as a business - sports - society etc) in a limitless fashion. Don't let your mind be stuck in the 3-D - move on to the higher spiritual realms and potential possibilities. Living out these lifetimes will help us eventually reach God-Like Love and abilities.

After my readings with Psychic Dove I began "seeing" some of my own past lives and/or receiving clues to some past lives. When I would receive a clue into my intuition, I called Psychic Caleb, Dove or Namath immediately in an effort to confirm my thoughts as well as my thinking. (Not once did any of them say that my intuitional thoughts and thinking didn't match up. In fact most were confirmed with and agreed with enthusiasm from my Psychic friends). For example, in the fall of 2021 I was hiking at Sedgwick County Park, where many of my intuitive connections with Peggy have taken place. Up to that point my intuitional meetings with Peggy were of her taking me "upstairs" to a higher realm with very high vibration! In fact, one time she dressed me up for a social event. My very cool "Apricot" Sports coat was the incredibly handsome! This is another example of Peggy's artistic tastes including fashion design as she has presented herself in classy workplace and social fashion. During my work years my suits might have a somewhat colorful dress shirt but I wouldn't have been caught dead in apricot or peach sports coat. This was so beautiful I kick myself now for not being more creative).

When I walk/hike I go fairly fast for an hour to an hour and a half. Almost every time there is a period of 10-25 minutes where I go into my "zen zone" where my brain waves are right for a message from my Peggy. This "zen-zone" is exactly the "zone" I used to get into during my jogging days which lasted for 25 years. We called this period our "runners-high" and for me, who used to jog on the streets, or in a park, the "runner's high" period was about the same time in length "20 minutes give or take a few" minutes, as my "zen-zone" was.

It is during the "zen-zone" or "runners high" period that my creative mind was(is) incredibly strong! During my YMCA administrative years problems would be solved, and/or creative management or program ideas would come to the front of my thoughts. Like a dream, I sometimes would need to stop and write down the details, before I would loose the creative though or creative ideas. On this particular day in the fall of 2021, I was walking by a chain-link fence that looked like a prison fence with barbed wire at the top. It reminded me of Steve McQueen and the movie "The Great Escape"! All of a sudden I went deep into my personnel history and realized that I was at an Auschwitz prison encampment as I saw Nazi signs everywhere and a creepy sad feeling took me over for a few moments. In fact I had several visions following this one, over the next few days, during my walk/hike and those visions were all peaceful mostly after the Nazi's left the Auschwitz camp. It must have been residual energy that let me see that "all was peaceful now".

So I called Psychic Caleb for a quick confirmation of my thoughts and visions of Auschwitz. A few days later I told Psychic Namath about this psychic experience and this was when I learned that Psychic Namath was our 4 year old daughter "Olga" and Peggy was "Agatha" and I was Oswald. Olga came out of Agatha and Oswald. Olga had "special powers" that the Nazi's were interested in ie Psychic abilities. This might have kept Olga and Agatha out of the gas chamber for a bit longer. I died after I might have escaped from my building on the way to

Attempt to save Olga and Agatha - I was shot down by the Nazi's. I think this might have been some time in 1942 or 1943. Olga and Agatha were later gassed to death. Psychic Namath, Olga, told me a couple of times of what a great mom Agatha was because she, Olga, was not afraid - even at Auschwitz starring at the Nazi's day in and day out. That is until the day came that they also were to die in the gas chamber from Hell.

I am guessing that Agatha and I, Oswald, we're in our early to mid twenties. My reasoning for this is because in my life previous to this, when I was Oswald Rayford-Brown, I was killed on the WWI battlefield fighting for England. I had been a fairly prominent Cricket "batsman" in the 1890's and early 1900's. My biography may be on Wikipedia with a 1903 picture! Peggy was a maid whose name I am not sure of yet, and we romanced in otherwise off-limits scenario of the PBS 1970's hit serial "Upstairs-Downstairs"! Apparently the lack of respect for English traditions in the "Upstairs-Downstairs" mold caused Oswald (yes 2 lifetimes I was named Oswald) Rayford-Brown to be killed on the battlefield, in WWI, by friendly fire - presumably for breaking with these English traditions.

Not long after my vision at Sedgwick County Park about our life at an Auschwitz Camp, I received another vision. While I was walking/hiking in the exact same location as the Auschwitz vision, I received a vision of being a part of the Zulu tribe in South Africa 300-400 years ago. Peggy was there with me and we learned the art and science of spiritual healing. I was not given our names but Peggy has, and it seems always has had, exceptionally strong healing powers! Much of her healing education came from this lifetime and another life we had in Egypt! That lifetime was 2,000 years ago and Peggy, as "Stella, was what would be termed today as a "Massage Therapist". Stella also had Physical Therapy and even medical skills! I was there in Egypt with Stella (even though I was not given my name in my visions) and my 3-4 visions of this place in time was extremely clear! It was beautiful of an incredibly modern (for its time) beautiful Bath House Health Club focused on wholistic health, (although I am sure with its spa might have encroached on acceptable/non-acceptable sexual activities once in a while). The facility had a covered roof with bamboo like walls that had several open window and ventilation areas! It was lit with big long attractive fire-sticks! The atmosphere was incredible!

Women of course, were second class citizens, but Peggy ie Stella, creative and business like in all of her lifetimes, had plenty of customers including me and as with most of our lifetimes, we fell in Love again! The last vision I had of this Health Spa was similar to my last vision of the Auschwitz Camp we were at, which was, after it had closed down. I understood the Auschwitz vision because the same hollowed ground was now at peace. With the Both-house Spa in Egypt, it was sad that such a happy, healthy flourishing place was now shut down even though it's building shell remained. It's the same melancholy sense I have when I visit where an old Baseball Field, Ballpark or Stadium used to exist - especially if I played there or watched a game as a fan. I still have not figured out why I was shown these visions of an earlier time, but I am sure, with the emotion I feel, they were part of my previous lives.

In the winter of 2021-2022 Peggy, during several of my readings with and through Psychics Namath, Dove and Caleb, encouraged to connect with Nancy Shobe, who is an author as well as a Psychic Medium. Earlier Barbara, of Lightworker Tarot and Oracle, had encouraged me to have a reading with Aleah Ames. This reading turned out to be a wonderful and detailed past life reading with Peggy ie Maree' and my ie Davi' about our life in France, where we fell in Love for the first time! I mentioned above that it was roughly 3,500 years ago! Now Peggy encourages me to check out my lifetime in Prague 350 years ago. Sadly, it was a life without Peggy, but it was a great life as I was a wealthy lawyer. I opened a lot of land and owned a lot of livestock and horses and employed many workers. Apparently, whenever the ruling order would begin treating the lower classes badly, I would be called into town for kind of a community forum. I apparently would convince the rulers to give the lower class and even peasants some rights by using diplomacy and compromise.

It is amazing and gratifying sometimes funny and often hysterical to realize some ironies of my past lives to my current life. For instance, I can hardly grow a blade of grass in the front yard comparing it to my many lives as a farmer in past lives. And in sports, I just don't get the allure of soccer, mainly because you don't have to use your hands and arms at all and your upper body very little. (While realizing and understanding the great skills with the legs and feet with endurance). Yet, along with being "an outstanding Cricket Playing batsman, I was a pretty fair soccer player in England also. I cannot ever imagine that? Then there's my fear of horses in this lifetime, although I do like to pet and talk to them, I just never in this lifetime, have ever wanted to ride one. Yet, in my Prague lifetime, I was an outstanding horseman and wrangler! Who da thunk it?

Apparently, many of our past life skills and talents and experience will transfer over into current and future lifetimes - as will most of our physical features. But some will not - mostly because of current life's lessons that we need to work on and to learn about. This is of course true for everyone as we review our lives and plan for our next life and lifetimes ahead.

So it is with my Peggy and the tarot person I viewed a few months ago. However there is a past life experience that is "seared into my memory as if it happened in this current lifetime"- a life experience we never forget - even if it was a few lifetimes ago. I am not quite sure what lifetime it was but this particular day had turned to dusk as it feels as though we were heading home after being downtown. Peggy was driving a flat bed horse and carriage set up hauling store bought goods and a horse team of 3 or 4 I believe. Suddenly it was almost dark and something spooked the horses and she could not get them to slow down. I was riding along beside her to the left just ahead of her on my horse and I could see out of the corner of my eye as the horses sped up, they veered a bit to the right and they went down a slight but sudden decline over a ditch. A couple of horses collapsed, the flat-bed over turned, and Peggy was caught in the bottom of everything - was seriously injured - passing away a few days later. As that vision came to me early in 2022, it was as if this incident had just happened a few days ago. It was so real and that sad to me. It was a horrific time in all of my lives to live through as our lives turned in an instant.

This "Spiritual Vision" was either a past vision, which I think that it was, but it also could have been a future vision? Peggy came to me as I was hiking by myself at the "Tallgrass Nature Preserve" between Council Grove and Strong City Kansas on Highway #177. It was a beautiful hot and humid day in July of 2022. It was the kind of day I loved to play baseball because you really loosen up all of your joint, muscles and tendons. Needless to say I am in the minority with that type of thinking. On this hike in the middle of the Flint Hills it feels as though I was in the middle of nowhere and it was easy to get into the "runner's high" intuitional feeling! Peggy was with me all of the way and it is at times like this when I feel that I could actually reach out and touch her - she feels that close and she actually is - all be it on a faster more comprehensive wave length! Oh how wonderful it would be to slip through a little hole in the next dimension to hold her hand and to hug her. If that little hole had appeared - I wouldn't have been surprised on this hot, humid fun day for me in the middle of nowhere!

Peggy was dressed to hike as she loves fashion with a down to earth style for whatever occasion presents itself. She is alway dignified, classy, playful, very beautiful and pretty which often spills over into a healthy wholesome version of "sexy"! Today on our hike she has brown hiking boots, short black socks that help show off her deeply tanned legs, with a soft cotton pastel shirt and shorts combination in colors that are from Heaven I have not seen before but have beginnings of light blue, amber, crème and jade. She looks like "a million" as Lee Dodson would say!

As our hike in the Flint Hills continued Peggy gradually worked her way to a 45 degree angle to my right what seemed as if she were 90 feet (the length of a baseline) from me. This positioning has me recalling a couple of other times this has happened - as if she is in a prime position to download intuitive images to me in order to connect with me at what I call my level of spiritual skills and skill set. Suddenly, I am so happy to be talking to my 3-4 year old daughter, whose dress might make me think it was out of the past, but her level of comprehension might be out of the future!?? My daughter was delightful and we had a wonderful and fun visit talking about everything under the sun! I could still see Peggy to my right at 45 degrees and 90 feet away but was fuzzy and not clear and not her face - which was pointed straight ahead. My daughter said that she missed me and couldn't wait until we would come together again! I got major "goosebumps" when she said that as she gave me a big hug and disappeared into the Flint Hills. This was an incredible vision and left me with such a glowing feel good feeling that is very difficult to describe. I know it was real by the definition of connecting through and with another dimension! Whether it was a vision out of the past or of the future or both - it certainly was real as so many other visions have been real since Peggy came back to me on April 28, 2020!

One of my most recent past life vision was also a future life vision! As I was giving blood to the Red Cross in January of 2022 at a local church, Peggy suddenly appears! The gym of this local church in Wichita was being used by the Red Cross for a blood drive and I was one of the first to donate. The Red Cross staff decided to play fun upbeat rock music from the 1970's - during the time Peggy and I were at Washburn! Peggy started dancing while I am hooked up to the blood donation apparatus! Before long some of my old friends connected with Peggy and or myself from Washburn University were having a dance! All of these folks had passed over in recent years and it was wonderful not only to see them but having fun with Peggy dancing! It was hilarious to know of all of my friends in spirit were having such an incredibly good time!

Chapter 8

Future Life Visions

Peggy kept insisting that what I was "seeing" was a future vision and not a past one and that all of these good friends, mentors, coaches and teammates would be in my life again! I was amazed and in awe that 1) I picked this up with my spiritual intuition and 2) that we can have such fun even when we are on the spiritual side! It was a real honor to have so many people show up in essence to say "Hi" and helped me feel even more comfortable and re-assured about our spiritual life after this life!

As much as I have enjoyed looking into my past lives, and thank goodness I am an onlooker viewing myself rather than an active participant at Auschwitz again, the Future Life visions are really bright, happy, modern and full of hope! In the fall of 2022 walking at Sedgwick County Park I had 3 really fun future life visions! The 1st one is that I am actually playing Major League Baseball in a stadium resembling Old Municipal Stadium in Kansas City with modern architecture and conveniences yet keeping with some of the old stadium traditions that have always made baseball unique! This first vision actually came to me several times and I am wearing the uniform number #28! The #28 has excellent spiritual meaning and I am practicing playing right field during batting practice! I think it is one of my first games if not the very first game. As I am practicing my right field play Peggy is in the stands maybe 100 or so feet from me and she is holding our first child of this lifetime! The child may be 2 weeks old and Peggy is proud and happy as am I looking up to see both of them there is incredible! Peggy is not going to stay long but she wanted me to see our beautiful child and it really gave me a lift as you can imagine. In essence I was fulfilling 2 dreams in 1 now playing Major League Baseball and married to Peggy living our young life with our new beautiful child!

Vision #2 in the fall of 2022 came soon after the first vision as it is immediately after a baseball season has ended and I am sore and tired after a long and grueling baseball season. So we are going to take a family drive in our family van for a weekend vacation it feels like. I am stretched out in the back seat sitting sideways. Peggy is sitting in the passenger seat in the front with the baby who appears close to walking. Someone is driving the family van as I never get to see him/her or see his/her face. There is a little baby platform in the middle as we are on our way for the weekend trip the baby is suddenly standing on a platform of some kind in between the first row and the second row of seats. The baby suddenly lets out a Loud "oooooooooopppppppssss" 2 or 3 times with the funniest look on her face! The smell begins to swell up in the family van and I am laughing so hard as I am in hysterics! Peggy has a calm and fun look on her face as she dutifully begins changing our daughters diaper and both Peggy and daughter are playful as I am despite the smell!

Not long after the first and second visions I am again on a hike at Cheney Lake in the morning! Our baby in this vision is about a year and a half and we are out to dance at a non-alcoholic non-smoking dance hall. In this public setting tonight, since I am not a good dancer at all, I am caring our baby through the dance hall as Peggy and friends and people dance for real. I get to serenade my 1 1/2 old daughter and people are so nice to say "hi" to her and give "hi-5's" for a quick second or 2 as Peggy and the rest of the attendees dancing "get down" that night. It is obvious, and I am bragging about that our daughter is "Daddy's Girl" tonight! That is until it is time for a diaper change at which time our daughter is now "Mommy's Girl"! Peggy is in such a good mood and just always floats with what is needed! But every so often she just needs to "GET DOWN Tonight"!

Soon after these visions I had several visions of our beautiful modern house and I hope it is of our next lifetime! This is a house that is extremely open with big huge windows - often open, bright happy colors that I cannot describe other than some of the colors are a form of orange, yellow, violet, green etc. The fabrics are that way also as our living style is also open to everyone including neighborhood friends and families! Our 3 kids are older Elementary ages Margaret, Charlie and nickname Bubba. Margaret may have been a bit developmentally delayed but was making great progress! Charlie is a scientist type in this vision and possibly anemic. Bubba is the youngest, the biggest and an extremely talented athlete and baseball player! A happy go lucky personality who is just good at everything he does - with the possible exception of studying? It is a wonderful environment that Peggy has been working on for quite sometime and an environment we are being rewarded for! Along with at least 2 shaggy dogs!

My baseball career is coming to the last years in this vision tied to everything it will have been a wonderful career! The goal of Peggy and myself is to celebrate our children and our neighborhood and give back through our foundation! There is so much good that always needs to be done and Peggy started the foundation in this vision during her child bearing years using her past life resources such as her achieved Business Administration Degree from Washburn University in 1978!

One of the emotions I will feel with this particular future lifetime is 1) having a Major League Baseball career - something I truly Love but one that always comes to an end during years normally associated with being in the "prime of our life" and 2) feeling a loss with the "empty nest" syndrome when our children grow up and flee the nest. However our Home Life Foundation will keep Peggy and I active, we will also adopt 2 less fortunate kids, and I will be involved in Little Leagues that focus on playing for Fun, everybody plays and every player is important! Peggy will be an incredible high vibrational force for children and family rights and will take on leadership roles as we get older! Yes this is a "Whopper of a Fun Vision" of at least one future vision!

One Saturday morning in the spring of 2021 I was in the sleepy state of almost waking up and is a wonderful time when Peggy comes to me a lot through my intuition! She is always dressed beautifully as we "talk" and transfer thoughts back and forth to one another! We talk about anything and everything a "Spiritual-Sex" is even on the table!! Mostly we visit about what is on my agenda, I ask questions attempting to verify what I think that I experienced yesterday through my intuition or through telepathic communication. 99% of the time my perception and my intuition and my telepathic communication is verified by Peggy in these early morning conversations some which I will attempt to verify again connection with Psychic Caleb, Psychic Namath, Psychic Dove, Light-worker Tarot and Oracle,

Vince at 7-D tarot, Katy Tarot, Aleah Ames and/or Nancy Shobe. I am proud of this network and have some very dedicated Spiritual experts to go along with my favorites listed on my "Spiritual Favorites" glossary at the end of our first book "A Love Story Between 2 Worlds". I am not only proud to be associated as well as spiritually guided by these wonderful people but give thanks for the incredible dedication and mission of each of these spiritual leaders!

So, as I am waking up on this Saturday morning I am suddenly in an atmosphere of a Golf Club (I am a terrible golfer and never developed a love of the sport that most of my friends have) and the 19th hole visiting with none other than Lou Gehrig! I quickly realize that I am in a conversation with the "Iron Horse" - the Great New York Yankee - and Yes the ALS Lou Gehrig. We are watching the Baseball Game on TV and talking about the game! I realize that there is a small part of me that is incredulous as well as I am hearing his voice and that we are talking! It is wonderful and I realize that he is enjoying the conversation as much as I am possibly because everyone he meets seems to be paralyzed at the thought of talking to such a human and baseball legend! I was relaxed even though I wanted to touch his road New York Yankee uniform simple but elegantly designed with Navy Blue "New York" a cross the from and a big number "4" on the back! Finally I said to myself - This is Lou Gehrig - the one and only "Lou Gehrig" or as my then 9 year old Little Leaguer in Little Rock told me - answering the report I gave him to give me a report on a famous player who wore his number, which happened to be "4"! Which young Michael Spradlin announced to me that "Lou Gregor" was a great player!

I then woke up slowly - pinching myself in the process of letting the dogs out. Wow "that was incredibly amazing" I was thinking to myself! I believed, had it confirmed by Psychic Caleb, and believe it to this day and always will!

One of the most unique visions that I have enjoyed was meeting (again) and visiting with Peggy, as she was in our former life in Egypt, ie, named "Stella" (see my earlier description). It was amazing to me to be able to observe that the boundaries of time and space are sometimes different on "the other side - ie the Spiritual Side". On one vision I observed Peggy, as she is now, visiting with, yes you guessed it, Stella! I asked Psychic Dove, who is an expert with helping people see and deal with their past lives, and she said it certainly is possible as somehow or another, we catch up with ourselves! We have to remember, Psychic Dove reminded me, that our current conscious state is just a part of who we are. We generally believe that there are 4 layers to our being at any given time - one of these is our "sub-conscious" mind - which most of us have heard about and know a bit about.

Well, in much the same scenario as I described above, I am waking up to a nice visit with another of my baseball heroes! It is Carl Yastrzemski, the amazing 1967 Triple Crown Winner of the Boston Red Sox! Yay - led the Red Sox in a way that most baseball experts agree, was even greater than his amazing Triple Crown numbers. Yaz's clutch hitting, fielding, throwing and base running were amazingly clutch in leading the Red Sox to overcome 100-1 odds winning the 10 team American League pennant dramatically on the last 2 days of the season!

The incredible is happening as I wake up, in my, what I call my "runners high or walkers high" state of mind - as I am visiting with the great Boston legend. As a 13 year old Yankee fan growing up in Topeka, Kansas, I did not have the natural bias Yankee and Boston fans have for each other in New England. Mickey Mantle and my Yankee heroes were fading as the cruel fates of baseball make a player seem old as they reach their early 30's. The last place Chicago Cubs of 1966 and recent years had first caught the "fancy" of my baseball buddies in 1967, when they incredibly vaulted into 1st place on July 4 th, even ahead of the powerful St Louis Cardinals. The Cubs finished 3rd in the 10 team National League in 1967 and seemed like a sure bet to be a contender in the next few years. The Red Sox rise came gradually as the American League race moved on after the All Star game. Suddenly the Red Sox won 10 in a row on a road trip and all of New England was there to greet them with a wonderful grass roots show of support at the airport early on August morning! It was described as the "Boston Team Party" but this was just the first of many to come as Yaz and the Red Sox magically forged what was called "The impossible Dream"! (2 years later the New York Mets forged the 2nd impossible dream by again beating 100-1 odds to Win-the 1969 World Series)!

Lou Gehrig passed away, as we all know, in 1941 tragically stricken by "ALS" at only 38 years of age after he set the incredible record of playing in 2,430 consecutive games! Carl Yastrzemski was still alive at 83 when my visit came through my intuition! My distinct intuitive feeling is that I was visiting with Carl Yastrzemski in the future! It was incredible as are my other, recent intuitive experiences! "My Peggy" is the catalyst and the recruiter of bringing family, friends and baseball heroes to me. I often "see" family members and friends on my daily walks/hikes and even met my great-grandfather who I was named after, waiting for me as I was driving through the McDonalds line early one morning! He made it a point to introduce himself, and encouraged me to believe my intuition, and most of all to trust myself and especially trust what Peggy was bringing to me! In fact, he told me not to mess this up because Peggy was quite a catch - and everyone Loved her on the "other-side"! I recognized him immediately from family pictures and my intuitive feeling I had at that moment; which was very early after I realized that Peggy came to me for sure on April 28, 2020.

One of the most amazing and awesome ways that Peggy communicates with me is through synchronicities! My early lessons when I initially sensed Peggy through my intuition is that we all have our own special and distinct vibration and we know each other's vibration intuitively! In the Spirit World that is how we know each other and communicate. Thus our own vibration which is as distinct and different (just like our finger-prints in the material 3-D world) knows those close to us as our subconscious kicks into gear! The feeling knowing that it was Peggy, even though she came "out of the blue" felt so familiar to my senses and I was ecstatic beyond belief! Never have I known such incredible Joy!

The lessons Peggy taught me about the Spiritual meaning of colors and numbers is "Ho-hum" to many Biblical experts, art historians and mathematicians. The fact that I never had a clue indicates what my math and art skill level is - at least in this lifetime. Beginning with the color "beige", which stands for being dependable, conservative and trustworthy, Peggy showed me this color for several days in high definition until I got the idea to look it up the information on what the color means and how it is defined. All of the connection of colors and numbers is found easily on you tube so I assume that I am almost the last one to figure this out.

Then Peggy showed me Amber and it = creativity and then pink which stands for unconditional Love then blue = loyalty and purple = experience among other things it can mean an "old soul". As I explained more thoroughly in the first book this was an amazing process with Peggy communication with me through my intuition and through telepathic communication. Peggy was attempting to explain to me her core values which were very similar to my core values. The core value I know about Peggy that is so similar to my parents is that she is smart, spiritual, quiet and low key within herself - all which in my mind = balanced. Even though Peggy and I are similar with these values I as an Aries can be much more pronounced, shall we say, and forthright with what I am thinking and with what my opinions are. Many Aries have this strength and weakness - and sometimes it gets us in trouble.

During the presidential election of 2020 I was visiting a friend on Election Day and Peggy was so worried and concerned about my mental health that she was coming through with incredible telepathic communication every 15 or 20 minutes! It was as if she was calling me on the telephone and it was also as if we had just fallen in Love for the first time! She was both Fun and Funny and I was so incredibly happy and yet so stunned! This Election Day was absolutely incredible!

I began noticing numbers on the clock in the 1990's and at first thought they were fun but incidental. I thought it was fun for instance to notices numbers like 3:17 or 3:53 as I would think of my all-time baseball hero Mickey Mantle. Mickeys best 2 seasons had batting averages of 317 and 353. It was when Bobby Murcer passed away of brain-cancer in 2008 and I began seeing 3:31 for his best batting average in 1971. Bobby took over Centerfield for Mickey Mantle in the great Yankees tradition and was a devout Christian and was always my 2nd favorite player of all time. I also began noticing other baseball averages and stats on license plates and the clock and Highway signs etc. Most of the time I will notice these numbers during periods of time when I am thinking about that person or that player. In 2018 I was moving from Alabama to Kansas and I was thinking about Bobby Murcer's rookie season in 1969 and how he jumped out to a great start leading the league with 43 rbi on Memorial Day when he badly sprained his ankle and never was the same for the rest of the year. So I am driving and realized that our motel is on highway#259 in Oklahoma as we had passed through Alabama and Mississippi and a bit of Arkansas. Well 259 is Bobby Murcer's batting average from his rookie season in 1969!

Peggy's Investigation has taken many additional twists and turns since the 1st book came out in August of 2022. The Good News is that law enforcement crime investigators have their collective eyes on Peggy's ex as well as the hired murderer. They believe that Peggy's ex hired the murderer because Peggy was becoming wise to the "black-market" business these 2 had gotten themselves into. From a military career to pharmaceutical sales and into a "black-market" business that included child and teen sex trafficking, liver and body part sales and transplants and just about any ugly entity that money could buy. The law enforcement and criminal investigators have been watching these 2 and who they interact with as they are mostly criminals themselves.

The new twist to Peggy's investigation is that a third major partner has been discovered. Originally the murderer had an accomplice that was a "look-out" in case something went wrong as the murder took place. The accomplice is real and has been talked to by law enforcement investigators but a MD in the Dallas metroplex area is being watched closely. It is now believed that Peggy was driven to Dallas by her ex for a health check-up. The MD gave Peggy a "slow-down" pill. Peggy, feeling disoriented, went outside and sat down outside on a park bench. Sadly that is when the murderer and accomplice snatched her up and killed her stashing her body in a poor part of the area. Later, Peggy's ex went back and cut up the body into small pieces and threw the body pieces and fragments away in a trash dumpster.

Now - it is up to the investigators to prove this and what they hope to do is to get more evidence and proof of more criminal behavior that Peggy's ex and murderer have been involved in. Apparently and sadly there is a lot of other criminal contacts that these murderers are connected with. Interestingly enough they have kept Peggy's I-Pad and credit cards and internet connections up to date so that it looks as though she is still alive in this world.

The Dallas area MD is extremely political and has a sparkling reputation so this part of the investigation could get very ugly and very sticky. Additionally, he is wealthy and Jewish, thus he has a lot of political clot but it appears that his relationship with Peggy's ex and her murderer, is one of many black-market type criminal offenses that the 3 have been a part of together. They have also been involved with many other criminals in separate criminal dealings and this is what law enforcement investigators are looking at with the attempt to connect many dots in many other cases.

I still believe in the old saying that "Cheaters never Win and Winers never cheat" even though it does not look that way sometimes. In my incredible spiritual journey with Peggy in the last 3 years, I am convinced that this old saying is more true now than ever. It may take a few lifetimes for people like Hitler or an Al Capone or even recent political leaders who appear to have sold their soul to the devil. I believe that they cheat themselves and the delicate balance of the conscious and sub-conscious mind first and foremost. Even in baseball steroid users gain an unfair advantage that their mind will constantly battle the rest of their lives. In the game of life the consequences can and usually are much more serious when involved with criminal activity. It will take many lifetimes for some people not only to learn but to rid themselves and in many instances family members of negative karma from past lives. A person may get by with criminal activities for a while but it will eat on their conscious mind in this lifetime and in future lifetimes.

This is why in my opinion, human beings need to "get out of our own minds" and have a much broader picture of the world we live in, who we share this beautiful planet earth with, and broaden our scope even into the universe, the multi-verse and into past and future lives! We are all here to do one thing: to learn and try to improve to be more God-like. Let's let go of old time man made rules and stipulations and let's move on to more full futuristic ideas and lessons that will help us grow so we can help those around us grow so we can connect with and support each other! And live happily ever after with friends, family and God!

Final Thoughts

This true story, A Love Story Between 2 Worlds is a captivating sequel to Charlie Lord's first book: *A Love Story Between Two Worlds.*

I have had the privilege of collaborating with Charlie Lord on the quest for justice for Peggy. We have become friends and I am proud of Charlie for sharing his personal story.

Charlie's intriguing autobiography is a decades-long journey beginning with his experience as a college athlete and major league hopeful, alongside his college sweetheart whose impact on Charlie's life during college was *only the beginning.*

Sports and cheerleading undoubtedly go together, and so did Charlie and Peggy. Beneath the surface of their lighthearted relationship was a deeply rooted friendship and admiration for one another. It's the type of connection that anyone would hope lasts a lifetime. This entertaining yet emotional deep dive into the complexities of Charlie's account of his college glory days, and quest to understand the events surrounding their separation, reveals a very personal and traumatic void created by the disappearance of Peggy.

Baseball lovers, past life theorists and spiritual seekers alike will agree that this soul connection is undeniable, and the events surrounding rediscovering each other was quite profound. My belief is that soul bonds are never broken, and love can endure the most difficult circumstances. This story will draw you into the heart-wrenching but heart-warming story of loss and reconnection. The exploration of past lives and current life circumstances come together in a whirlwind of a story!

Life has a way of throwing curve-balls at us, and this is certainly one of those accounts. When you believe life will unfold one way but rather it takes a drastic turn, it can raise more questions than answers. Through it all Charlie's optimism and quest for truth would lead him on a wild ride of theories, psychic insights, and a surprising continuation of what was once thought lost.

Barbara Hurst
Psychic & Medium
Author: *From Darkness to the Light [Confronting Soul Wounding]*

Updated Spiritual Reference List

1. The Bible
2. The Power of Positive Thinking by Norman Vincent Peale
3. Around the Year with Emmet Fox
4. The Twelve Powers by Charles and Cora Fillmore
5. Light from Many Lamps by Lillian Eichler Watson
6. Science and Health a Key to the Scriptures by Mary Baker Eddy
7. The Scole Experiment by Grant and Jane Solomon
8. Life after Life by Raymond Moody
9. Numerology by Michelle Buchanan
10. Ask your Spirit Guides by Sonia Choquette
11. Magical Things and the big book of Angel Tarot by Radleigh Valentine
12. Who's Who in the Bible by Philip Comfort and Walter A Elwell
13. Adventures of the Soul by James Van Praagh
14. Wisdom from your Spirit Guides by James Van Praagh
15. The Power of Love by James Van Praagh
16. Heal Yourself - Heal the World by Deborah King
17. Episcopal Church Book of Common Prayer
18. Your Life in Color by Dougall Fraser
19. California Psychics on the WWW
20. Lightworker Tarot and Oracle
21. Katy Tarot powerful psychic readings
22. Melanie Beckler inspirational spiritual meditations, videos and books
23. Two Mystics Tarot powerful Psychic readings
24. Psychic Ann of Wichita, Kansas
25. The Education of a Baseball Player by Mickey Mantle
26. The Glory of their times by Lawrence Ritter
27. Daily Word and Unity Prayer Ministry - Unity Village, Missouri
28. Around the Year with Emmet Fox

29. Sermon on the Mount by Emmet Fox
30. Spiritual Economics by Eric Butterworth
31. The Positive Principle Today by Norman Vincent Peale
32. Explosion - Mickey Mantle's Homeruns by Mark Gallagher

"Build a little fence of trust around today;
Fill the space with loving words,
And Theron stay;
Look not through the sheltering bars
Upon tomorrow,
God will help thee hear what comes
Of joy or sorrow".
Mary Frances Bult

Printed in the United States
by Baker & Taylor Publisher Services